Desires of a
Prodigal Daughter

Desires of a Prodigal Daughter

INSPIRATIONAL TRUE STORY

TRACY V. JAGGI

TREASURED WORKS

Dedication

*To my husband, children, grandchildren,
family, friends, ward family, community,
and angels, both seen and unseen.
Thank you for your love, aid and support.
You are all a part of my journey.*

Contents

Re·con·cep·tion – *a new or different idea of what something or someone is like, or a new or different basic understanding of a situation or a principle.*

Con·ver·sion – *the process of changing or causing something to change from one form to another.*

Con·tent – *in a state of peaceful happiness.*

Prod·i·gal – *a person who leaves home and behaves recklessly, but later makes a repentant return.*

Special Thanks

FIRST AND FOREMOST, I will thank my wonderful husband, Scott. He has supported me in my highs and lifted me from my lows. He encourages me to be my best self. His God given ability to seek the good and always stay positive is inspiring. His ability to step to the side and let me tell my version, from my perspective, knowing his story would read much differently. For allowing me to release every human emotion as I compiled and relived fifty-one years, over and over, processing and articulating it. Many times, he questioned if my book was helping or hindering, as he watched me write, laugh and cry.

My amazing children, grandchildren and their families. I am in awe of them and their many qualities including their resilience, and their love, assistance, service and support of me. They are all blessings in my life and bring me great joy.

My brother and his family, for validation and venting. Nothing I could say adequately describes the love and appreciation I have for them and the role they hold in my life; I carry them in my heart, thoughts and prayers.

My dad and step mom, for their hardworking examples—although we would like a do-over, we are grateful for second chances, forgiveness and the ability to keep moving forward.

My in-laws for their faithful dedication to the gospel and their family. For being two of the first people to read my book in its early stages and discovering many shocking things about me—later admitting that it would be hard to show how far I had traveled if I were unwilling to disclose half the distance.

My extended family, thank you for your love, support, advice and examples throughout my life. You have all contributed to my learning and growth.

My mother with her unconditional love and faith in her Savior Jesus Christ—through ALL of the good, bad and ugly. I would not be me without her.

My oldest daughter, Saxen, you were the motivation I needed to get my life on track. You have endured many versions of me and my book, having both lived it and re-reading it multiple times, editing and revising. Thank you for being the first influence in getting everything worked out, in both areas.

To my friend and aunt, Sonya Buckner, with your bold opinions, assertiveness and ability to speak your mind and know exactly what you want while waiting patiently to acquire it. Your quiet confidence standing before God and our tender spiritual, gospel related discussions and application to trials and life. Your Christ-like ability to love others; you are a great example of what it looks like to be a faithful Daughter of God.

All of my friends, including Amy Rogers, Candice Rollins, Andrea Packer, Kitty Vercimak, Susan Woody and Sharity Beck. I love and admire you all. I am so honored that our paths have intertwined and appreciate our varying points of view—all which have allowed me to expand my understanding. Thank you, friends, for sharing your journey with me.

Until recently, Janice Walker Lyman, you were an unrecognized angel. We have been friends for many years without much effort or acknowledgement of the role we played in each other's lives; taking each other for granted. It wasn't until compiling my story that I realized how many times you were there, in pivotal moments. Because of this experience and interaction with my book we have been able to recognize divine intervention and have enjoyed meaningful, in-depth conversations that we *never* had before. Thank you for your encouragement, assistance and feedback throughout this exciting, scary process.

To Richard Paul Evans and his family at Author Ready, Diane Glad, Kim Autrey, Francine Platt and others behind the scenes. Thank you for your time, effort, abilities and expertise in the field and your willingness to share them, encourage and create such an array of amazing authors and books. Especially Debbie Rasmussen, author and editor, I have enjoyed working with and getting to know you, thank you for holding my hand throughout this entire process.

Two of my once, very close cousins, Michelle Fogg, M.S, founder of Utah Food Allery Network and Cody "TexnArtist" Walker, I love you both even though we are miles apart and busy with life. I know I can reach out for your advice, assistance and honest opinions, even if we disagree.

Thank you to new friends and fellow authors, Rosilee Barreto, Celeste Edmunds, Kathleen Rose and Mary Flint, for your support and encouragement to push through the hard and remind me why I started this process to begin with—to use my experiences, to lift and inspire others—that we may overcome this mortal life with all of its difficulties; we can turn to God and assist each other along the way—to remind everyone that no matter what we have experienced we each have a story to tell and we are *not* alone.

DESIRES OF A PRODIGAL DAUGHTER

Thank you in advance to my readers. It is my hope that my journey may inspire you, in even the smallest of ways, as you continue pushing forward on your own path. From this moment forward we can walk, crawl, inch, dance, or wander together.

Above all, thanks be to God, Jesus Christ and the Holy Ghost. Without them none of this would be possible. But with them, I am everything I need to be—*I am enough.*

Introduction

⁓

FROM A YOUNG AGE I have enjoyed writing poems, stories, and journaling. Writing has been a way to process my feelings. I have always written in spurts, but the blank pages were there waiting for me to fill them with stories, thoughts, and experiences, when I made the time to do so.

For years I have planned to write a book. I knew the title, contents, and have been collecting information and quotes. But the hour to write hadn't come yet.

In the midst of many struggles in 2023, I strongly felt inspired that it was time. I started writing my planned book, but then I ran across this quote:

"Desire denotes a real longing or craving. The doctrinal teachings concerning desire, relate so directly to our moral agency and our individuality. Whether in their conception or expression, our desires profoundly affect the use of our moral agency. Of course, our genes, circumstances, and environments matter very much, and they shape us significantly. God thus takes into merciful account not only our desires and our performance, but also the degrees of difficulty which our varied circumstances impose upon us." *~Neal A. Maxwell of the Quorum of the Twelve Apostles of The Church of Jesus Christ of Latter-day Saints.*

That quote became my new jumping off point, and inspiration took over. I changed my direction and focus. I saved my other ideas for later and began with my life story.

Many years ago, sharing my experiences would have freaked me out. I was not ready, but I am now. You may be familiar with the parable of the prodigal son as found in The Holy Bible in Luke Chapter Fifteen. A son desired his inheritance, left his family, squandered his birthright with riotous living, and found himself in the dung eating with the swine. He finally came to himself and returned to his father where he was met from afar off and greeted with the finest robe, the fatted calf, music, and dancing. His brother was angry that after years of faithfulness he had never received such a celebration. His father responded, "...be glad: for this thy brother was dead, and is alive again; and was lost, and is found." ~*Holy Bible Luke: 15:32.*

This classic parable from the Bible gives me hope, because my life resembles it. I am a prodigal daughter. I took the comfort and safety of my home for granted. I was spiritually dead but am alive again. I was lost, but now I am found. I was living in darkness but now I see and feel the light. If you're struggling to navigate your life's challenges, I urge you to ask the Spirit to testify of the truth, as you read my story—that you may feel inspired.

Through the gospel lens, I have come to understand that our Father in Heaven is worried less about where we've been, or where we are, rather, He is more concerned about where we are going. I know where I have been, where I am, and where I want to end up. I learned that my desires determined my direction. Allow me to show you a glimpse into my story; my journey, away from—then back to my Heavenly Father. Not once, but again and again.

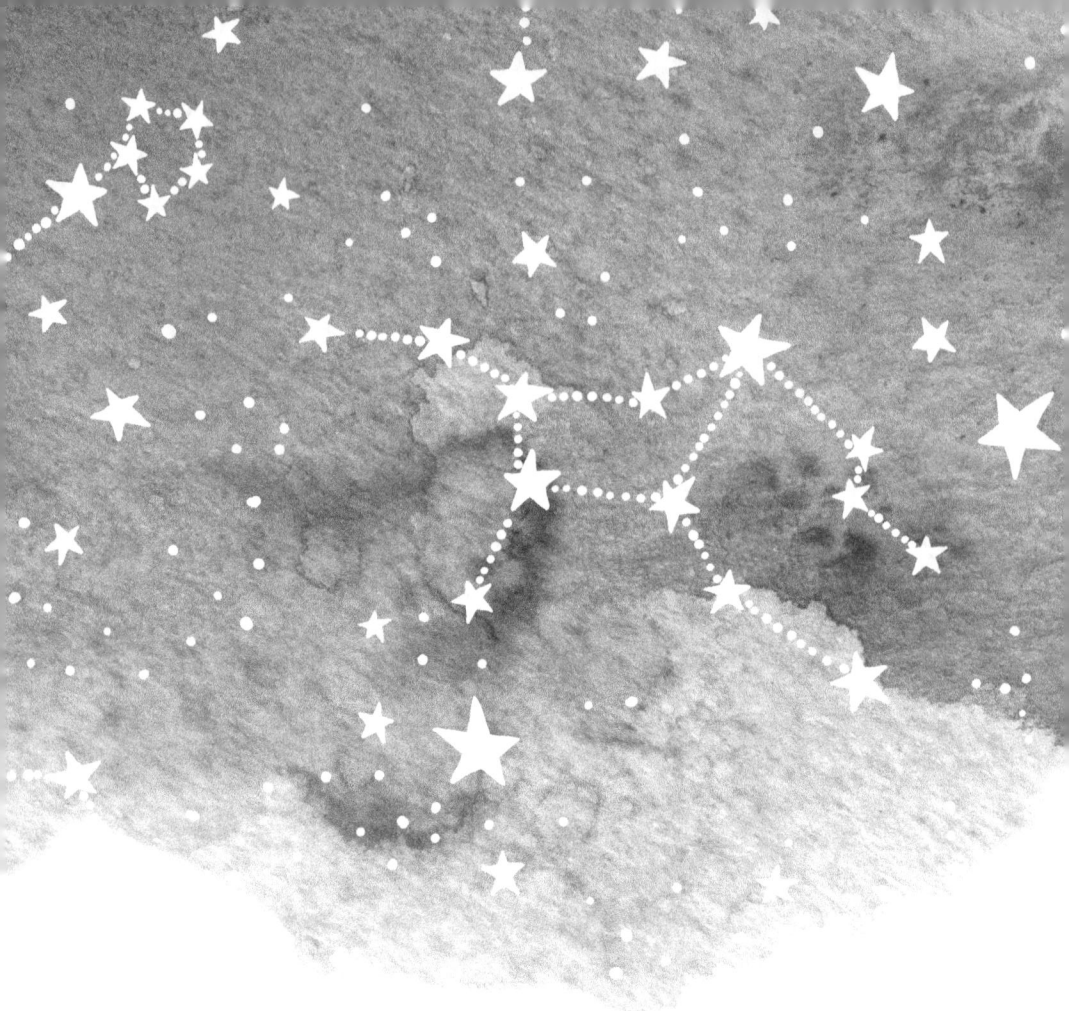

Con·cep·tion

The forming or devising
of a plan or idea (s).

CHAPTER ONE

My Family

*B*EING A GIRL, I always felt like I was a disappointment to my parents. From as young as I can remember, I was told that I was supposed to be a boy. My name Tracy was the boy's name they picked out for me.

Surprise! I'm a girl. However, they decided that name worked for a girl, and instead of Vance for my middle name (if I had been a boy), I'm Tracy V. I hated my name. It was a constant reminder that they planned on a boy. However, the V did allow me to pretend that I could have been a Veronica or a Victoria.

I tried to act like a boy sometimes, or what I thought boys acted like. I tried to be "tomboyish." But I was actually very sensitive and girly; I failed at suppressing it. I felt bad when I did "girl" things. I wished I was a boy. I came to believe that being a boy, or at least a "tomboy," would have been better.

Only adding to my belief, my annoying, adorable, younger brother, Michael, was spoiled and could do no wrong. He would antagonize my sister and me, and we would get in trouble. He would hit us multiple times, and when we would hit him back, he would cry, and Mom's response was always, "What did you do to your brother?" He would sneer in delight as we were punished. We would be left to babysit, and if he did not complete his assigned chores, it was our fault. My sister Terri and I got to the point where we just did his work for him to spare ourselves the physical or verbal abuse.

One time, he randomly removed the handle from the push sweeper and split my head open with it. I can't recall my mother's response. Another time, he launched a gun off the porch. I was his target, and the butt of the gun hit me square in the face, breaking my nose. As usual, from Mom, "Be nice to your sister." I was jealous of him because he never had consequences and seemed to be loved more than me.

My older sister was awesome, and I looked up to her. She was outgoing, friendly, and confident. I considered her a tomboy. Terri rode pedal bikes, skateboards, motorcycles, and could burp the alphabet. Our dad was a Tae-Kwon-Do instructor, and like him, she loved the sport, earning her black belt.

I only took one class, and Dad took me to the front to demonstrate a move. I hated it! I never went back. I did not like being in front of people. The one thing I did like was riding motorcycles, though I did not drive too fast. I was afraid of getting hurt.

Terri was not afraid of anything. She welcomed the thrill. She seemed excited when she split her chin open as a result of jumping her bike off a cinder block covered with a four-foot by two-foot piece of plywood. Her gash continued to grow when she kept talking and talking on the way to get stitches. She also took pride in showing off her twelve-inch scar on her abdomen from accidentally swallowing a sewing pin. At one point, she was in a hip-to-toe cast because she jumped a skateboard and broke her leg. I recall the canary yellow rubber boot she was required to wear to protect the cast when she showered. She was full of life, energy, and was everything I was not.

I idolized her.

The first house I can remember living in was in Green River, Wyoming. I was almost four years old. It had a peach and brown exterior, with the front door facing east. Upon entering it, off to the right, was the living room. I have a memory of celebrating Christmas there with the tree decorated in colorful lights with lots of ornaments and tinsel. A hallway opening was on the south wall of the living room leading to the bathroom, which was the first door on the right, and the bedrooms were at the end of the hall. From the front door you could look straight into the kitchen.

Once, my grandpa Virg was sitting at the kitchen table, my sister and I were getting out of the bathtub, and we were wearing our terry cloth nightgowns which doubled as towels. Mine had a large pelican on it. We sneaked down the hall and peeked around the corner, and Grandpa roared and scared us. We laughed and screamed and ran back and forth from the table to the bedroom several times. Michael was a baby, and our delightful loud noises startled him.

There were two doors in the kitchen, one at the end of the cabinets on the north wall that opened to the garage. We had a litter of puppies get into the insulation in the garage and pass away in there; that made me sad. The door at the end of the table on the south wall led down to the unfinished basement. I would play with my Slinky as it flipped from one raw wood stair to the next. I followed my Fisher Price train while it drove around on the concrete floor and played music from the plastic record of my choice. I enjoyed the music. My father was on shift work and did not appreciate our daytime rowdiness that woke him while he tried to sleep.

The house was elevated on a corner lot with a sloped yard. We would roll in the grass and down the hill toward the sidewalk. One time, Terri split her eyebrow open doing just that. It bled really bad, and it scared me. I was sad when on the road to the north, Waggles, our dog, got run over. I hated losing our animals.

My dad was born on the tenth anniversary of the Pearl Harbor attack. He is the second of five children. My grandma, Merlin, moved back to Lyman, Wyoming, the summer before her senior year and after Christmas started dating my grandpa, Clinton Walker. They soon fell in love, and following graduation they got married on August 11, 1947. Grandma was seventeen, and Grandpa was nineteen years old.

The oldest of five children, my mother, Paula, was born in August of 1954. When her parents met on a Friday afternoon at a local barn dance, my grandma, Kenna Sue, was fifteen and my grandpa, Virgil McMickell, was twenty-one. They went out again on Saturday and after a four-day courtship, they were married on Monday, December 17, 1951. I was often told their whirlwind love story throughout my life.

My parents' story was much the same. Dad was seventeen, Mom was fifteen, like their mothers. I was always told that Grandpa Clinton informed them they could not get married unless there was a reason. So, they created a reason, a baby. Mom dropped out of school in the tenth grade to start raising my sister Terri. Dad went on to graduate from high school. They had three children, each of us three years apart.

As the middle child, I was not old enough to do big sister stuff, and I was not young enough to get away with everything like my baby brother. I felt like I was left out and did not fit in. I adored playing with my Barbies, Strawberry Shortcakes,

Cabbage Patch dolls, and my Care Bears, the popular toys then. I collected tea bags and would hide them in my drawers like scented sachets, because I liked how they smelled.

My favorite aroma is Christmas; to me it smells like cinnamon and hope, if hope has a smell. In an attempt to hold onto the glimmer of Christmas all year long, I saved shiny silver tinsel that fell from the tree. One of my dearest Christmas presents was my Easy Bake microwave. I enjoyed countless hours of baking and serving my desserts. I had a favorite cookbook that was made up of all sepia writing and illustrations. It included step-by-step instructions for things like cinnamon sugar toast and loaded baked potatoes. When I was eleven years old, my grandma Sue showed me how to make pie crust from scratch, without a recipe. As I said, I was very girly, yet in the back of my mind, I just believed that something was wrong with me. I was not enough. If I could only be different, I would somehow be better and more loved, like my brother and sister were.

We were always told that kids were to be seen and not heard. "If we fart, we'll put it in a jar and save it for you," was another favorite quote. It was used when we were excused from adult activities. I never actually got any fart-filled jars. I did get backhanded, yelled at, constantly called stupid, and told I was in the way. I despised having my ears pulled and having my dad's thumb buried in my collarbone, which both happened often. My parents struggled with their marriage, and as a result, my dad would leave almost yearly. Early on, my parents divorced, then remarried. Years later, they were sealed in the Salt Lake City Temple of The Church of Jesus Christ of Latter-day Saints.

I vividly remember the day we were sealed. As an eight-year-old, the beauty of the temple fascinated me. In the dressing room were fancy vanities with lighted mirrors, which made me feel like a princess. While we waited to join our parents in the sealing room, I laced yarn around hole punched greeting cards. Kind, attentive women dressed in white escorted us through the large halls to be with our parents. I can still see the sage green velvet altar, fabric chairs, and two large mirrors adorned with gold trim that hung directly across from each other, showing our reflections going on for eternity. I recall how I felt, peaceful.

However, that feeling didn't last long, and even a temple marriage did not keep my dad from leaving. Without fail, Mom would sit us down and tell us, "Dad is leaving; he does not love us anymore."

CHAPTER TWO

The Good Life

*B*UT LIFE WASN'T ALL BAD, some parts were good and fun. We laughed, played, ate well, crafted, sewed, baked, watched TV, played cards, dice and video games, went to Lagoon, water parks, and Cherry Hill. We rode motorcycles, explored, treasure hunted, fished, listened to music, and danced.

My dad was serious about martial arts. He was a first-degree black belt instructor. He owned swords and nun chucks and could do the Chinese Splits. We watched Bruce Lee movies and spent time with the families of students in his classes.

Most of Dad's family were horse people, but he preferred motorcycles. My only horse memory with my dad happened when I was very young; it was a Sunday, because I was in my church dress. We were in his parents' yard, and at the south edge of their property was a swift canal that disappeared into a large culvert under the road. My dad decided to cross the canal right in front of the culvert where the horse, my dad, and I were all buried under water.

I was scared to death and didn't care to ride horses after that. I had a lot of fears, but riding on a motorcycle with my dad was not one of them. I felt safe on the back of his bike, with him in control. He was very skilled and athletic. I couldn't wait to feel the wind in my hair and the freedom you can only get while riding.

Dad had a passion for treasure hunting. He read books on the subject and purchased a metal detector and tools. I vaguely remember him going on a couple of trips to the Grand Canyon in search of riches. My mom went with him once, and they brought us kids back souvenirs. My sister and I got Grand Canyon Fred Flintstone shirts, and my brother a Barney Rubble one. In addition, us girls received Native American beaded doll necklaces, while my brother got a tall, bamboo handled, rubber tipped spear with feathers. We were in heaven.

My dad sought after gold, or artifacts, that if found, promised great wealth. I recall going on a few treasure hunting trips with caves and climbing involved. One trip, there was a huge hole and no way to walk around, so my dad did the splits over that hole, and we walked across his legs to get to the other side. I was naive about how impressive that was and to the monetary value of things, as most children are. As a result, I was happy with finding coins, old bottles, petrified skulls, and interesting rocks. I enjoyed following my dad on our family adventures.

My mother was very talented and delighted in cooking, sewing, crafting, and dancing. We had a large console stereo with a record player, an eight-track cassette player, and an AM/FM radio. She exposed us to several different genres and eras of music. I think back to singing along and dancing around with each other, without my dad, and often with my aunts and cousins. I loved it. It was one of the times we were free, and it was acceptable for us to be loud, fun, and silly. We also crafted and painted with my mom creating works of art. Once I made a big pink hat with a floral arrangement on it, which was meant to hang on the wall, not be worn. We painted Artex wall hangings, tablecloths, and dish towels. She taught me how to sew; she was generous with her time and talents.

Mom was an amazing cook, a great seamstress, florist, and decorator. She would reiterate lessons learned from her middle school home economics teacher. We didn't dine out much, but when we did, I drank the miniature cups of half and half and licked the individual slices of butter after carefully peeling off one side of the paper. She planned and prepared meals, and we ate extremely well. Most dinners felt like a holiday or special occasion. She used to tuck little gifts and trinkets like Avon necklaces and collector pins into our napkins. It was always a wonderful surprise. I can't even begin to count how many times I was told, "We can make that cheaper," whether it was food, clothing, or home decor. Upon request, she whipped up a dress only two or three days before a church dance. It was a black and mint green cocktail dress and one of my favorites. I later loaned it to a friend to wear and never got it back. My first prom dress was also handmade. It was a yellow satin with a matte yellow floral pattern, three-quarter sleeve, sweetheart neckline, form fitting, and tea length with a peplum.

Mother sewed less when we moved to the motel. We lived in the house built for the manager. It was the same house my grandma and grandpa Walker used to live in when they managed the motel years prior to us. I have fond memories when they worked there of watching Saturday morning cartoons and Grandma feeding us pancakes. Years later, when we moved in, it still had the same brown paneling and cream wallpaper with taupe and gold ornate vertical stripes. Our kitchen was where my grandma Sue showed me how to make pies. While living there, I received my first Cabbage Patch doll and where us kids liked to hide in the large walk-in closet. My great-grandma Marell, Grandma Sue's mom, would come stay with us and almost empty the soaps and lotions out of our bottles to fill her empty containers she premeditatedly packed. She was always kind enough to fill ours back up with water in hopes that we would not catch on to her little scheme. It was one of her many quirky habits.

Terri, Michael, and I liked to play with the motel room keys and would leave the house using the long secret passageway that exited out the back by the laundromat. My sister and I had jobs washing and folding the guest towels. A man exposed himself to us one day while doing laundry. Our parents never found out. They were also not aware of the *Playboy* magazine's we would find in the maids' closets when we were putting the towels away.

I have a lot of memories at that motel. My favorite was my sister and I getting dresses, *store bought* dresses. My pink chiffon Easter dress had a high lace-trimmed neckline and long sleeves. I wore it to church a few times. Terri's was a beautiful floor-length lavender gown, with sheer sleeves, and a high collared sheer lace neck with a V-shaped ruffle. It had a dark purple satin ribbon that wrapped around the waistline and hung down the length of the gown in the back. She wore that dress a few times as well. One time was to her freshman prom, and another time she wore it to a funeral.

I still wonder where most of my beloved clothes and other belongings ended up. I long for a few special items I once owned. I suppose there's a slight chance my mother still has them…somewhere. Mom has hung onto many of the items and decor that once adorned our homes. I can still picture the layout, colors, and decorations of all our houses.

The one we lived in the longest was our leaky single-wide trailer, which had been relocated several times. It found its final resting place on a one-acre piece of property down the "dugway" of our hometown.

The front door led straight into the living room. At the east end of the trailer was a bedroom with a corner angled ensuite and a small closet. That was my mom and dad's room. The kitchen was open to the living room. The olive-green fridge, sink, and stove were all on the south wall along with a window above the sink that faced the larger side of our property where we carved out a dirt track with our motorcycles. My mom could watch us out the window and see the dugway leading uptown. Terri and I could look out and dream of anything other than doing dishes. It seems like we did a lot of dishes. Oftentimes, our punishments included removing every dish from every cupboard, hand washing, drying, and putting them all back perfectly.

A wall separated the front of the house. The front being three-quarters of the kitchen, the living room, and the master suite. The back being the laundry, pantry, hall, two bedrooms, a full bath, a large and small storage closet. The washer, dryer, and small closet were on the backside of the partition wall. Next to the closet on the north wall was the backdoor leading out to the burn barrels and two sheds that sat at the far north-west corner of our property. Our land was backed by bulky railroad tie corrals arranged between us and the highway. That highway led to Interstate 80.

Across from the laundry nook were large bifold doors hiding the pantry. Between the pantry and the backdoor was the start of the long-zigzagged hallway where my dad used to commence yelling at us to get our asses out of bed. He would repeat this morning greeting all the way down the hall, his volume increasing as he got closer. The goal was to get out of bed before he arrived. Prior to entering mine and Terri's room, he would pass Michael's smaller room, which at one point had two framed pieces of artwork on the wall. They were of sad Artex clowns painted in the "seventies" colors; orange, olive-green, brown, and yellow. Separating our rooms was the full bath across from the large storage closet, again with the bifold doors.

Finally, he reached our shared bedroom at the back of the trailer. It had one large walk-through closet with two doors, a window that opened and faced the same way as the kitchen window, and a large bay window with a west view of the corrals. In the window seal sat a white vinyl pad where we shoved our display of dolls and stuffed animals. We had two beds, a dresser, and a white shower curtain thumbtacked to the frame where our bedroom door used to be.

At one point, Terri and I both had velvet bedspreads. One was a deep crimson red and the other a crystal ice blue with matching fringe, the same distinct color as our uncle Michael Dee's eyes, my mom's second brother. We had an Artex wall hanging of a hobo holding a flower with the words, "God does not make junk" painted in neon colors. We had a lot of hand-crafted items, as my grandma and Mom used to sell Artex, Avon, Tupperware, and Tiara glassware at different times throughout my childhood.

My favorite decorations were from the early eighties. Light green Tiara glass dishes, canisters, and a clock, paired with strawberry wallpaper and various strawberry decor and knickknacks proudly displayed in an old soda crate, painted red, and all hung on the partition wall in the kitchen. I loved that kitchen. On the same wall hung a red rotary phone, with an extra-long spiral cord that allowed us to hide on the other side of the wall by the laundry and pretend that the sound of the dryer would muffle our secret conversations. Occasionally, I would get all twisted up in that cord. My mother would politely answer that red phone, even if it interrupted her yelling and screaming at us kids. Later, Mom changed the kitchen from strawberries to white geese wearing bonnets with accents of yellow and smoky blue. I questioned my mother's mental stability. Really, geese in bonnets?

The TV, the console stereo, a couch, loveseat, and ottoman were in the living room. They were cream tweed with chocolate brown and country blue plaid. When we sat on the right side of the couch, we could see a perfect circle on the top of the headrest that had been there for years. A lamp had tipped over cauterizing the fabric and exposing the yellow foam.

We had a few lamp episodes. The most memorable was my dad flying his new zip-pull toy helicopter he received for Christmas. It spun out of control and crashed into a lamp. However, it was a separate lamp incident that I can't fully recall that melted the couch. I can perfectly call to mind barely turning twelve and being asked to sit on that couch. That tweed, injured, once cozy, forever burned in my memory couch, where my most uncomfortable experience took place.

I was eleven when my mom joined a self-help group called, "Good Life." I went with her to a local meeting. All I remember is that they played the new eighties song, "We are the World," sung by a variety of popular artists at the time. One of them was Michael Jackson. I was a fan of his music and dancing. I even owned silver sparkle socks, suspenders, and a glove. I would wear them and dance and sing along to his music, privately in my room of course. Mom would go down to Salt Lake City for a few days at a time to attend their workshops. I think my sister went once or twice as well. The next year I ended up going down to participate in the actual course. Even then, we were all searching for it, a *good life*.

It was no surprise when my sister confided in me that she was going to run away with her boyfriend. Her bag was bright yellow with an emerald-green young women's emblem and drawstring (the youth group for girls in The Church of Jesus Christ of Latter-day Saints). It was packed and hidden in our closet. I wanted one of us to get out. I had saved up some money from babysitting and folding laundry, so I gave it to her for her escape. She told me she loved me and that she would miss me, and that soon she would be making a break for it. Leaving our life for a good life, I thought. And of course, she asked me to keep it a secret. I kept secrets well.

Terri and I always celebrated our birthdays together. They were three years and four days apart. Terri's was September 10, and mine is September 14. We were usually given the same thing but different colors such as one pink and one purple big-eyed Bradley doll. One year after my relentless complaining, we finally got different gifts. I received a Big Bird metal lunch box with a thermos. I was so disappointed. I can't even recollect what her gift was, I only know I wanted it instead. The next year, we went back to getting the same different colored gifts.

In September 1985, my sister turned fifteen and I turned twelve. We were recently living down the dugway in our relocated single-wide. It was the beginning of her sophomore year, and I started the seventh grade. Our family fought a lot; Contention lived in our home and interfered in our relationships. It seemed Contention was a member of the family.

On Sunday, September 29, my sister woke me up with a hug and asked, "Let's not fight today," and I agreed. We had plans to hang out as a family, instead, my parents left to go shooting and must have taken Contention with them. Us three kids stayed home alone with our assigned duties. We got along unusually well that day.

My parents returned in the late afternoon, and that evening we watched a movie. I have no recollection of the movie other than it had adult situations, and when the situations came up, the children were excused. We would retreat to our rooms; when the scene was over, we were invited to return. Michael and I went back out to continue the movie, but Terri stayed in our room to do her homework. The next time we were dismissed, I sauntered back to our bedroom. When I arrived, the white shower curtain was thumbtacked back up from the inside. We had been fighting and yelling with Dad again, and Terri slammed the door, so he removed it for us. We hung the curtain for some form of privacy; it had been our temporary door for a while. However, it was short, so it did not reach all the way to the floor. I carefully crawled under the curtain to find the south window open and the room empty. I knew my sister had made her escape, but I checked the bathroom just in case; she was not in there either. I returned to the living room safeguarding her secret. About thirty minutes later, my brother announced that Terri was gone. I knew I was going to be in trouble.

Dad later discovered that his little .22 caliber pistol was missing as well. Terri had snuck it out of his sock drawer and taken it with her. Cops, friends, family, and her boyfriend were called. Small search parties were sent out to look for her. I woke up in the middle of the night relieved that they had found her, as she was once again comfortably sleeping in her bed. To my surprise, the next morning, it was not her. It was one of her friends that had been out helping look for her.

Several tense hours later, Michael and I were asked to sit down on our wounded couch. I watched through the sheers as my parents slowly ascended the porch stairs, opened the front door, and sat with us. The words were heavy on my ears and heart. They had found Terri's body. My world stopped turning, the shock set in, and the sobs broke out.

I was devastated. —It wasn't true, it couldn't be true.

CHAPTER THREE

School Years

I MISSED SCHOOL THAT DAY and many days after that. When I did attend, it didn't seem important. I fit in less than usual. Kids would ask me insensitive questions. One boy, named Jeff, asked me, "Is it true that your sister was found in a trash can, cut up in little pieces?"

Who asks those kinds of questions? Underdeveloped, inconsiderate, middle schoolers, that's who. My mom was worried about me, so I was pulled into the counselor's office for his comfort and wisdom. He informed me that, "I would get over it." I was angry, resentful, and heartbroken. I didn't want to get over it, I just wanted my sister back. My attendance and grades suffered more than usual that year. As a result, we had to petition the district for a grade level advancement. Under the circumstances, it was granted.

I never really liked school. For kindergarten, my class was in the south corner of a blue metal-sided building. I did like the cinnamon graham crackers we dunked in milk, and the green Martian the teacher used to help us learn our alphabet, but my teacher was mean and abusive. I was scared of her. Along with other children, I was hit over the head with big heavy books.

She also duct-taped a girl's mouth and placed her in the corner for talking too much. I didn't talk much.

I was shy and quiet even at home. During this time, I remember staying in a single-wide south of the Maverik. The kitchen was at the front of the trailer and the rooms at the back. I looked forward to having my grandma Sue come visit and wearing my favorite red dress that she gave me, with raised, white felt miniature polka dots. Overtop was a white, eyelet lace apron. It was the dress I wore for my school picture that year.

I blocked out most of the first grade as, yet again, I had a mean, abusive teacher. The only thing I recall is asking to go to the bathroom, but instead, I ran away from school. I was almost at our trailer on Sage Street when I heard police sirens and assumed they were after me, so I hid in the bushes across from my house and waited most of the day. It took a while for my teacher to notice that I never came back to class. They went and got my sister out of her grade to inquire as to my whereabouts. I later emerged from my hiding place, but the aftermath escapes me.

At home Mom moved the furniture around a lot as we played outside in the grass. I would peel dandelion stems in half and place them in water and watch them curl. Michael and I would unwrap Crayola crayons and melt them in the heater vents. Terri and I tattled on a boy we witnessed stealing a small drawstring bag of gold nugget chewing gum from the local IGA.

We moved three times when I was in the second grade. I started in Lyman, Wyoming, then soon moved to Vernal, Utah. We were there for trick-or-treating. We went to a neighbor's house and felt spaghetti noodle brains and peeled grape eyeballs. I still can't eat mushy grapes. I kept a half-full pillowcase of candy in the top of my closet and ate out of it for months.

I had one of my scariest dreams living in our single-wide home that we relocated there. My dream was vivid and real, the kind that wakes you up in a sweaty panic. My uncle forced me to wear a gory full mask. I resisted, but he was stronger than me. I struggled to tear it off, but it became fused to my face. I was traumatized by that dream as if it actually happened.

Christmas in Vernal was better, no bad dreams. My brother received a Fisher Price two-level toy car garage with a ramp and car elevator. My sister and I got Barbies and several handmade Barbie and Ken outfits.

I have many memories of me, Jet and RJ, two boys from school, walking up a wide ramp from the lunchroom to get up to our classroom in the multi-level school building. Every morning, we said the Pledge of Allegiance and swished our mouths out with mouthwash that was poured into miniature paper cups and carefully placed at the corner of our desks. We sang "Do-Re-Mi" as a large group in the auditorium or the gym. I can still see the little *Dick and Jane* picture books we used to read.

By Valentine's Day we had moved back to Green River, Wyoming. My teacher was an Asian woman; she wasn't mean. Our neighbor's daughter got lost after school one day. She had diabetes and had got on the wrong bus. Her mom panicked while drilling me for answers, making it seem that I was responsible for the mix-up.

We lived in some apartments with a park in the center. I was afraid of a man that used to hang out there. He resembled a specific singer; I am not sure how I made that connection, but that is what has been imprinted in my mind. The road between the apartment and the park was a hill, and I wrecked my pink, Huffy pedal bike going down it.

While living there we had a cat that liked to keep her new kittens in a frisbee under my bed. I also watched my sister as she was thrown over the back of the tweed plaid loveseat and kicked in the stomach a few times while on her hands and knees. I never knew what she did to deserve it.

We were already back in Lyman for me to start the third grade. My teacher was tall and intimidating. Mom was the room mother and helped with all the school parties. I had a hard time with spelling and started to learn cursive. My two front teeth had grown back in; they were huge and sideways. I could fit two or three quarters in the gap between them. I would go to speech therapy in one of the small portable single-room trailers they had parked outside of the blue school building. I attended with a boy that shared my name. The speech therapist had very thin hair exposing the majority of her scalp, but she was kind.

At this time, we were living next to my grandma and grandpa Walker. It was a doublewide on the south side of the canal that ran the length of both properties. The same canal I was submerged in years before with my dad and Grandpa's palomino horse. Our rental had a galley kitchen down the center. The bedrooms were at the back, where I accidentally dropped one of my younger, squirmy cousins on his head while in my room.

One of my aunts and uncles gave me a good scare when I was opening a gift from them in our living room. They had strategically shoved a large stuffed frog into a tiny box. Upon opening the package, the frog leaped out at me. I jumped and screamed. That scary frog became one of my closest friends; he slept with me and comforted me for years.

Fourth grade was awful. I attended the newly built school in Urie, Wyoming, and had a first-year teacher that looked like the wicked witch from the *Wizard of OZ*, without the green skin. She was mean and frightening. I wet my pants in her class because she refused to let me go to the bathroom. We had relocated our single-wide again; this time to the trailer park on the east end of town. My sister and I were sharing the middle, smaller room. We had bunk beds and a dresser. One day, I tried to jump up on the top bunk, catching myself with both fists gripping the bedding. Unfortunately, the covers started to slide off the bed. I landed with one foot on the floor and the other on the corner of a dresser drawer that had been pulled out and was sitting on the floor. I cut my foot and needed stitches, crutches, and had to elevate it for weeks. The witch would not allow me to raise my foot even with a doctor's note. The doctor told my mom that if the cut was ¼ cm deeper, it would have severed the main tendon in my foot.

For my school picture that year, I wore a smoky blue, long sleeve shirt with a ruffle on each shoulder, paired with tan, corduroy bibs and a blue Smurf shoelace tied around a small pigtail in my hair.

Fifth grade was my favorite. We still lived in the trailer park. My dad brought a gigantic bag home from work. It was made from tightly woven trampoline-type fabric that could hold air. We sat it just off the west side of the porch. One kid would sit on the far end while another one would jump off the porch onto the bag, launching the sitting child high into the air. We spent hours jumping and flying off of that airbag. That was the same porch where my brother threw the gun off and broke my nose. I have a distinct memory of a Native American man standing on that porch; my dad was not very happy about it—I didn't know why.

That year, the police arrested a father for keeping his two children chained up in a trailer not far from my walking path to school. It was the first time I had a male teacher, and he was so nice. He had a glass eye and a soft voice. We did leather stamping that year making keychains, bracelets, and belts. I took an empty, washed, glass barbeque bottle to school and covered it with several torn pieces of masking tape and stained it with brown shoe polish. It was the vase that held tissue paper flowers we crafted for our moms. I fell off the monkey bars hurting my ribs and ripping a hole in my new, black corduroy pants. A kid in our grade wrecked while tobogganing; he came and visited the kids at school while in a full body cast that covered everything except his head and hands. This same year was the first time I had a best friend.

We were living at the motel for my sixth-grade year. The workers that were regular guests there would flip beer caps from the second-floor balcony and pay Terri and me to pick them up from the parking lot so they could do it all over again, night after night. Some of the 1984 Olympians traveled through our area and stayed at the motel, gifting us with red, white, and blue Olympic winter beanies. I was introduced to a lot at the motel and school.

A new schedule structure started that year. We had a home-room teacher for most of the day, then switched to different teachers for a few subjects. Meditation was taught; I found it very stressful. We were required to be quiet, but I needed to cough. I was so distracted focusing on staying silent, I almost choked trying to keep from coughing. It was awful. This was the magic year we were separated by gender, and each watched our own maturation video. It was awkward, and I was embarrassed. Girls were starting to develop, though I was not one of them. I noticed that a classmate of mine had only five outfits, one for each day of the week. Every Monday, she wore the same ensemble, every Tuesday, and so on for the entire year. I had my first boyfriend in the sixth grade; he broke up with me during recess after three or four days. My best friend moved to Rock Springs, Wyoming, and I went to stay with her family for a few days. We went shopping at the mall and bought matching painter hats splattered with bright colors, but after that, we didn't stay in touch.

Lyman had recently built a new high school, so the old one became the middle school, and I went there for seventh grade. It was on Main Street and just across the road was the "Merk," the local grocery store. We would walk there and get Jolly Rancher sticks. They came in peach, caramel, cherry, and pink lemonade. They probably had more flavors, but those were my favorites.

We got lockers and a different teacher for every subject. I started to feel cool and grown-up as a middle schooler. That didn't last long for me. Because my sister had died, it didn't feel cool when everyone stared at me when I walked down the hall. It wasn't cool when I was asked to leave a school dance because good grades were required for eligibility, and I was not eligible. It wasn't cool to feel lost, alone, and sad. I had a few friends that I hung out with. Somehow with their help, I managed to survive that year, when we buried my sister.

I noticeably started to develop in eighth grade. Mom was taking me down to Salt Lake for some of the Good Life seminars. Those trips would usually include shopping at the malls and buying me the latest on sale 80's fashions. Our small town was a bit behind in the trends department, so I may have stood out from the crowd. My outfits were a good cover up and distraction. Maybe if they were looking at my clothes, they wouldn't see right through me. Hopefully, they would start seeing someone other than the girl whose sister died. My outfits never concealed the low grades I earned. I was not a behavior problem, just a poor student. I never got in trouble for my bad grades at home; my parents didn't seem to care. Unlike a kid in my science class, whose mom would come to school and sit behind him if he had a failing grade. She would whack him in the back of the head if he even thought about "dinking" around.

Speaking of "dinking" around, this was the same year that while grocery shopping in Evanston with my mom and Grandma Sue at the IGA supermarket, our bagger boy insisted on pushing our cart and transferring our items from the cart to the car. Soon after merging onto the freeway to head home, an older single cab pickup sped up just ahead of us. We had a front row seat to our bagger boy climbing out of the driver's side window as his passenger slid in under him to take the wheel. He went out of that window, across the bed of the truck, and back in the cab through the passenger window, showing off, while the truck maintained sixty-five miles per hour. They proceeded to follow us thirty-eight miles home where he was shocked to learn that I was only thirteen years old.

Even at that age, Mom taught me how to drive a stick shift, and I soon started making deliveries for her floral shop. While out on a delivery, I was pulled over, and after inquiring about my driving skills, the officer said my driving was not the issue. He made me park the truck and drove me to the shop where he strongly encouraged my mother to hire a delivery driver with a license. He knew our family and that I was not old enough to be operating a vehicle.

My freshman year was located at the newly built high school. I continued to ride the bus after getting busted for underage driving. My sister would have been a senior that year, and I often held my breath in anticipation of her appearance in the halls with all of her friends and classmates; she never showed up. I think her peers felt sorry for me, and I was probably a reminder of her loss for them as well.

I went to watch the Jets perform at the Utah County Fair; it was my first concert. I failed English that year, as I had such anxiety about public speaking. My other grades were barely passing. A handful of girls hated me, and at that time for class fundraisers, they would sell the freshman as "slaves" to the upperclassmen. I was scared of who would buy me and what they were going to make me do. I felt relieved when an attractive boy I liked bought me and only made me carry his books a few times at school, until the end of the week when he insisted on giving me a ride home.

I was too scared and embarrassed to say anything about his version, because his story of what took place was very different from mine. I endured a couple of grade levels overshadowed by him, and I continued to feel enslaved until his graduation set me free, kind of. I had a great deal of practice at pretending and keeping secrets, that experience just got added to the list. Prom was toward the end of the year, and arrangements were made for me to meet a friend there. I wore my handmade satin yellow dress and purchased a solo prom photo to capture the experience. My mom even made me a matching yellow rose wrist corsage. I was grateful to have made it through my first year of high school.

My sophomore year was neutral, not good or bad, just different. With my sister's class graduating, the atmosphere changed, friends shifted. Earning poor grades continued, and I failed math. I still mostly hated school; however, it was a nice break from home. I was fifteen now, and my grandma and Mom were both married at fifteen. I was obsessed with wanting to know who my husband would be, so I tried on several last names. My notebooks included many versions of Tracy & so and so, carving initials into binders, paper, and skin. That year at the New Year's dance, I wore the handmade black and mint cocktail dress, and I found him, the one I wanted to spend forever with. We began going steady, and I fell in love quickly. He attended our rival school, and I was occasionally harassed for wearing his letterman jacket with their school colors. It didn't stop me from wearing it to school for the next two and half years. I liked being someone's girlfriend rather than the girl whose sister died.

Our broken family drove to Galveston, Texas, that year. It was the only actual vacation we ever took together not including camping, fishing, or Cherry Hill. While we were there, Mom and I found a baby blue, satin, strapless, three-tiered, tea length dress for my school's prom with matching jewelry and a pink metallic, floor length, strapless gown for my boyfriend's Junior prom. They were both on sale of course, and my mom could not have made them cheaper.

I anticipated my junior year being great. I was going to get my license and finally be able to drive, legally. Even though I was an experienced driver, I failed my first driver's test. I was extremely nervous and intimidated by the scary female driving instructor. My second try was successful, and I was able to drive myself to school that year. I had two jobs—babysitting and working at Taco Time. Along with buying my own motor-cycle, queen size waterbed, several clothes, and other items, I had saved enough money to make an agreement with my parents to pay one-half the cost of a used, spray painted, blue Trans-Am. They would pay the other half; my dad was just as excited as I was.

My attempt again at public speaking ended in disaster but not a failing grade. I am sure the teacher took pity on me as my demonstration speech oozed orange smoothy out of every crack from the one broken blender loaned to me by the Home Eco-nomics teacher. It was not intentional, in fact, she was one of my favorite teachers. Not only was she wonderful, but I also liked the subject content—baking, childcare, and interior design.

My mom threw me a sweet sixteen party held at my grandma and grandpa Walker's house. Mom made her famous oriental meal, and we ate with chopsticks. It was a fun time, but the best part was that I could officially date. The "rule" was that I had to be sixteen, but my mom was very lenient with the rules, as long as we kept it a secret from my dad. Proms had been the exception because they were special.

My junior prom was all the things a high school girl hoped for. My mother paid a ridiculous amount for my black sequined, strapless, form fitting, mermaid gown with a hot pink bow, hidden tulle, shoes, gloves, and jewelry. She made me a huge matching hot pink and black wrist corsage at her floral shop. Add the crown from being voted first runner up for prom queen and I felt like a princess.

However, I did not feel like royalty later that night when my boyfriend got me very drunk for the first time ever. He had soaked slices of fruit in fruit punch and alcohol for weeks in anticipation. The jungle juice was terrible, but not as bad going down as it was coming back up. I didn't like it. My boy-friend's senior prom that year was the one and only time he told me that I was beautiful. I remember slowly dancing to a song, "Lady in Red" while wearing my red dress with draping fabric around the shoulders and fitted ruched fabric that was long in back and gathered up at the hip above the thigh high slit. Although I no longer had to keep dating a secret, I had started participating in other activities I definitely didn't want my parents to find out about.

I got a late start to my senior year, as out of concern, my mother admitted my brother, herself, and me into a counseling facility down in Orem, Utah. I was finally released about three weeks into school already starting. Dad was gone for good, and Mom was only there physically.

Mom said Dad had our utilities shut off, and I had to go to the neighbors to shower and get ready for school. It was humiliating and inconvenient. I decided to go live with my dad while he was living with his parents. It didn't last long as it was evident that his new girlfriend was his top priority, so I went to live with my boyfriend's mother. She was also divorced and working; my boyfriend was away at college, and his sister was busy with several high school activities, so I was usually alone with his mom. I learned a lot from her, and she got me through my senior year. Somehow my dad ended up with my Trans-Am in the divorce, so she let me drive her car. I actually got good grades my senior year and was eligible to participate in school activities. I was five feet eleven inches and encouraged by a few high school coaches to play volleyball or basketball, but I had no desire to.

My life was not like the other students my age. I attended my senior prom in my beautiful red dress, recycled from the previous year. By some miracle, I barely managed to scrape by with all of the necessary requirements; I proudly received the honor of being one of the first to graduate from high school on my mom's side of the family. At seventeen years old, I accepted my diploma in my black cap and gown. I was the only girl to wear black, after some mix-up with the ordering. All the boys in black and all the girls in royal blue, except for me. I felt different, I *was* different, so it was appropriate that I wore black. To mourn my life, my loss, my school years, my childhood, my despair, and bury my secrets.

CHAPTER FOUR

Secrets

WHILE GROWING UP, I wanted to spend time with my Grandma and Grandpa McMickell. They were fun and they loved me. They smoked and drank coffee from sunup to sundown. I often tried smoking crayons, pretzel sticks, and candy cigarettes. They would sneak me coffee even though my mom was opposed to it. When I was probably fourteen or so, with my grandma Sue in Vernal, we went and visited an elderly woman. She complimented me on my physical beauty but then gave a disclaimer that, "pretty is as pretty does." I knew I was not pretty; I had done ugly things. For years, her words affected the way I felt about myself. All the bad things that happened continued piling up, and the reflection in the mirror became more and more unattractive. I lacked confidence and self-esteem. I wanted to believe people when they told me I was pretty, but I couldn't. I knew and felt all the ugly on the inside. Like Julia Roberts said in the movie *Pretty Woman*, "the bad stuff is easier to believe."

After my sister died, I kept most of her clothes and items intact and felt very protective over her things. I knew she wasn't coming back for them and trying to hang on to her and all her belongings did not help me feel less alone. Isolating myself from the rest of the family probably didn't help either, but we didn't mention my sister much. Somehow it seemed off limits and made everyone sad. There became an even bigger disconnect between us after her passing. When I did leave my room, I could feel the tension squeezing me. Things were different when my dad was at work or gone—they were worse. Mom was frantic most days. One time she happened to be holding a knife in her state and threatened to kill me with it. My mind flipped through my recent behavior to make a mental note as to what may have triggered her. She and I yelled and screamed at each other; we told each other to "F" off frequently.

Michael and I would always fight. One time he yelled at me while standing in front of the washer and dryer, "I wish you would have died instead of Terri."

I replied, "So do I, brother, so do I."

I didn't just say it—I longed for it too. I believed that God got it wrong. I had a few dreams at a young age with Jesus holding me on his lap and telling me everything would be okay. Those dreams got me through many hard times, but not this. He lied, I was not okay, it was never going to be okay ever again. If God wasn't so oblivious, He would have taken me. I loved God and Jesus, I was spiritual, quiet, shy, and reserved. I wanted to live in heaven, I hated my earth life, I wanted to go home. My sister loved life. I thought she got along better with Michael and our parents. She was fun, outgoing, active, and she deserved to keep living, not me. I was angry and distraught. I did not know much about the dealings of God, but I was convinced that if He knew what He was doing, He would not have sent me to my family. He would not have given me a crap life, and He would have taken me instead of my sister.

It was my fault she was gone. If I had told Mom and Dad, Terri left the house when I discovered her missing, she would not have had a thirty-minute head start, and we would have found her alive. I was the reason she was dead. When I gave her my twenty-three dollars to help her run away, I would never have dreamed in a million years that she was going to die. I thought she and her boyfriend would get married and live a good, happy life. After all, she was fifteen, old enough to get married and have kids like my mom and Grandma.

I could not tell anyone, they would blame me, everyone would hate me more. I already hated me enough for everyone. I punished myself with guilt and shame. I would stay in my room and cry, dance, and sing to my music. I memorized the lyrics to, "Don't Cry Out Loud" by Melissa Manchester. I would repeat it again and again. Ironically, I cried as I sang. I tried to do as the song directed, keeping my sad feelings and tears on the inside, unless I was alone in my room. Eventually, that's what I did. I shoved everything down, with the exception of anger, I had a hard time hiding that emotion. If I didn't talk about it, maybe it would go away. If I hid my feelings, they would go away. Maybe if I pretended to be okay, I would be. Maybe, one day, like the wise school counselor advised, *I would just get over it.*

I spent as much time in my room as possible, I could cry in there. My mother needed to know my whereabouts at all times, she was a freak about it. Cleaning was an acceptable activity, so I cleaned my room all the time. I would take everything out of the closet and the dressers. I would sort, iron, fold, organize, clean, and put away while singing, dancing, and often crying. I was able to drag this process out for four or five days at a time. I would then spend a day or so out of my room before

I would dump everything in a huge pile on my bed and start all over again. I just kept cleaning my room again and again. It was my escape from the rest of the house and the people in it. I hated walking past the small closet between the laundry and the back door. That closet was where Mom kept the evidence box from my sister's crime scene. I didn't want to see it, but I knew Terri's items were in there, including her shirt with the bullet hole and her blood.

My mother always kept a lot of stuff in the house. It was what we were used to, but our home was organized and clean, I thought. Mom insisted on things being done exactly right. If the laundry wasn't folded just so, we would have to redo it. If dishes were not spotless, as previously mentioned, every dish came out of every cupboard and redone. If she was not pleased with the tops of stands or dressers, everything was cleared off in one fail swoop onto the floor, and we started over. The toilet paper needed to roll off the front, or else. Terri or I could vacuum the whole house, and Mom would find the one spec that was missed, and we would be in trouble. We were backhanded, yelled at, threatened, called names, and were drug around by our ears. We could never do anything right. I sang "I am a Child of God" a few times and wondered why my parents were not kind and dear?

God must have loved me less than other children.

Before Terri passed away, Mom went missing for a few days. They finally found her curled up in one of the back sheds sleeping; she hid out there for two days, presumably. I heard whispering of a mental breakdown, although I didn't know what that was. All I knew was that it added to my worry for my mom. I felt it was my job to try to protect her and do things perfectly so she would not be upset with me all the time.

The winter after my sister was shot and killed, someone climbed across the cattle guard corrals, leaving footprints in the snow toward the sheds, where our large, blue eyed, white Samoyed Husky was stolen. We later found his body in a river; our dog had been drowned. We were always aware that an eyewitness identified my sister wearing a specific coat, but it was never found with all of her other belongings. After the snow melted and we could access the same shed where we found my mom, we discovered Terri's missing coat, thrown on top of the boxes. Mysteriously that winter, someone returned it to the shed; we figured they used stealing the dog as a distraction.

After Terri's funeral, Mom didn't get out of bed much for a while. I prepared most of the Thanksgiving dinner that year, including the pies. For Christmas, I received my presents and more, probably the gifts intended for my sister. Christmas didn't feel or smell like hope. When Mom finally drug herself out of bed, she spent weeks at a time in Vernal with her family, leaving me to take care of Michael, Dad, and the house. When Mom was around, she would badmouth Dad and point out his many flaws and provide details from his indiscretions. I never understood why she stayed with him. She believed, therefore, I believed that she was the victim. She always reminded me how much she loved him, her kids, and that she was extremely forgiving. I loved my dad and strived to earn his love in return. I loved my mom and knew she loved me, but I did not respect her. If she was stronger, she could have spared us from great pain. I felt she was a rug and allowed everyone to walk all over her, including me. I told myself I would not let others take advantage of me, that I would never be my mother.

I was already a victim though, having previously been taken advantage of. Desensitized to danger and conditioned to be seen and not heard, I was never taught how to advocate for myself. I did not have a voice, other than one in my head that was too scared to speak up. I didn't want or ask for things to happen, but they did. Bad things occurred, that's just how it was. Abusive mother, absentee father, mean teachers, inappropriate men, accidental R rated encounters, a dead sister, pushy boys, controlling boyfriend, spiked drinks, divorced parents, and the persuasive "family friend" that offered to take my senior portraits, free of charge.

I felt we lived a double life, one way when Dad was home and another when he was gone. I'm pretty sure he was unaware of what took place in his absence. We were instructed to keep things from him; other stuff I just didn't bother to mention. Life was better when Dad was home, aside from his own added issues. He was extremely intimidating with much less abuse than my mother dished out. He still had his unique punishment practices. The thumb buried in the collarbone may not seem like a big deal, but it hurt, as did getting whacked with the nun chucks a few times. Knowing his skill level in the martial arts was a very domineering way to keep us lined out. The most humiliating was one time when Dad agreed that my friend could have a sleepover and also go to the dance. However, after she came to stay the night, he decided I should only do one or the other, so we dropped my friend off at the church by herself and later returned to retrieve her. I hated having witnesses, as it made it harder to pretend that I was okay. She got to enjoy the dance while I hid in my room crying; waiting for her. Dad was more subtle than Mom, except when I was allowed to go to activities, he would pick me up right out front and lay on the horn—there was nothing subtle about that.

Several days after Terri's funeral, her spirit came and sat next to me while I was lying in bed. She told me I was going to be all right. I didn't believe her, and I begged her not to leave me. My sister looked exquisite and peaceful; much like she did while lying in her metallic lavender casket, it matched her beautiful lavender freshman prom dress she was laid to rest in. Her cold hands, with bruised knuckles, gently crossed at her waist just under the purple satin ribbon. The coroner told my grandpa that she fought for her life. I remember feeling the lumps and dents on her skull through her short, wavy, brown hair. The night she ran away, a relative picked her up and gave her a ride. He dropped her off at the end of our cousin's road where she told him she was planning on visiting. However, when he looked in the rearview mirror, she was still walking down highway 413.

Terri's body was discovered about a half mile from that very spot. She was found in the gutter across from the Gas-N-Go, just off the freeway. The string that held her broken red checkered sunglasses around her neck was down around her waist. Her black purse was in the road, and the gun was a ways off in the field. We were told it had a bloody fingerprint on it, but her hands had no blood or gunpowder. She had a single .22 caliber gunshot wound to her abdomen that Mom told me later took her over forty-five minutes to bleed to death from. Her clean Levi jacket was buttoned up over her royal blue sleeveless sweater to conceal the wound. Her clothes and white high-top shoes were covered in dirt from an assumed ground struggle; bruises on her knuckles were evidence of a fight, and the earth was disturbed all around the area. Even though local farmers had driven past the gutter that morning and testified she was not there, indicating the body had been dumped, law enforcement investigated it as a possible homicide but later ruled it as an accidental self-inflicted death. Many people thought she had killed herself, that is one scenario, but that is never what I believed. I did believe people felt sorry for me, as I did for myself; I could feel their pity and awkwardness around me.

My dad left us every year until I was twelve, but he always came back. Mom never missed an opportunity to tell us that, "He did not love us anymore." After Terri died, he stuck around for three strained years. Until one Sunday when my mom, my brother, and I returned home from a weekend visit with my mom's friend in Utah. We entered our house only to find my dad and all his belongings gone. I knew this time he was never coming back.

Prior to my dad's final departure, both of my parents ended up finding out about me and my boyfriend. It was humiliating to say the least. Dad was not happy about it, and I was the subject of many of my parents' arguments. I later concluded that it was a factor in his disappearing altogether. Although I contributed to the contention and discontent with my family, I was never in any trouble at school. I would never have behaved in public the way I did at home. It was like I was two different people. I'm sure if you inquired about me, everyone would report that I was coping quite well, with the exception of two occasions. The first one being when I told an overbearing mother to back the "F" up, it was not her junior prom. I was in charge of the decorations for prom, and she was trying to take over, and I was not having it. The second occasion when the hateful, angry me emerged, I told a leader to "F" off at Young Women's Camp, not my shining moment. I liked to use the "F" word. It was rebellious, and sometimes to get my point across, I knew of no other powerful word.

Before my complete inactivity from church, I only went here and there; every talk felt as if it were just for me. I was certain everyone could tell that I was a fraud, pretending to be better than I actually was. If they knew all the things about me, they would not want me there. I felt more guilty at church. I learned that I didn't belong. The other girls thought they were better than me, and I agreed with them. I'm sure they were glad to get rid of me. I was ashamed of myself, my life, our leaky trailer, my parents, of things that I let happen, especially that thirty-minute head start I gave my sister. Everything was my fault. I was angry with God, and I hated myself and my crappy life. If I could just hide, maybe I would not be found. My subconscious plan worked. Not only did I hide from people but from God. I stopped talking to Him, I didn't ask for His counsel. Why would I? He didn't know what He was doing. I moved far away from Him and turned numb to the Spirit. I was left in the dark, just me and the voices in my head.

My extracurriculars were the topic of many conversations with my therapist at the counseling facility. He told me that because I had premarital relations, that I would also be a cheater. Mom insisted we go and get help with the divorce and Terri's death, but my therapist was hyper focused on the fact that I was having sex with my boyfriend, it's all he wanted to discuss; he was creepy. My boyfriend and my aunt and uncle wanted to break me out after my many unfavorable reports about the place. But Mom was manipulative and managed to extend our stay. I didn't understand what the major issue was. A sixteen-year-old having sex with her boyfriend. I was in love with him, and I wanted him to love me. He said he wouldn't know if he loved me until after we had sex. Oh, how I wanted to be loved by him. Besides, my grandma was already married by this age as was my mom—with a kid. Several of my friends were doing it, I did not see the big deal.

I hated our small town; everyone was in everybody's business. I longed for a change of scenery and to replace the people around me. I could not wait to escape. I dreamed that my ticket out of town could have been to be a model, given the fact that I wasn't smart or rich and I hated school. Several people believed I was physically attractive. Mom found a modeling school down in Utah that recruited me for my height and beauty and signed me up. She would drive me down to classes that taught about makeup application, how to walk the catwalk in heels, photoshoots, and on camera commercial auditions, that's the part that terrified me.

A friend drove with us once and waited with my mom because we were going to walk around the fair after my class. The modeling school invited her to sign up for lessons, she was prettier than some of the girls attending. One girl definitely stood out as someone you would not think belonged there. Later, I overheard management talking about the fact that they would allow anyone as long as they were willing to pay the entrance fees. I didn't have much confidence that I should be there prior to that, but lost all confidence that I belonged there after overhearing that conversation. They didn't believe I was model material, they just wanted our money, so I quit. Conveniently, it also got me out of public speaking.

One of my uncles believed I could be a model. He dabbled in photography and shot photos of me and did our family portraits as well. He was the same uncle that would use his large stature to straddle me, pin me down, and put his tongue in my mouth when I was young. I guess it was okay as it was done out in the open and in front of my mom, even though I never liked it; she never stopped it. Not only did she not stop bad things from happening, she was usually the cause of them.

Money was tight, and tension was still high with my parents' divorce. Mom and Dad couldn't agree on who was responsible for what when it came to items I needed for graduation. Mom made arrangements with the family friend that offered to take my senior portraits. He tried to persuade me that I could be a model and convinced me that he had connections that would make all my dreams come true. Mom and his wife were upstairs, and I hoped that they were oblivious to the fact that he slowly and skillfully beguiled me to pose topless for some photos in his basement studio.

My boyfriend was my refuge. I only wanted to be with him, and I dreamt of the possibilities of a better life. He was smart and popular. He had a plan for his future, and I was included in his plan. I waited for him and passed on opportunities to go out with friends, attend activities, and even skipped my senior sneak. He would assure me that I would never find anyone better than him. He did not like the idea of me being a model. I was flattered that he didn't want to share me with the world. He reminded me that I would be in over my head after I confided in him about my coerced senior photo session. I agreed with all his assessments and was happy to follow his lead.

CHAPTER FIVE

The Plan

WHILE GROWING UP, I was told I was stupid a lot and I believed it. I graduated at seventeen; thought college was for wealthy or smart people, and I was neither. Although I was working, I started wearing out my welcome with my boyfriend's family. I accidentally wrecked his mother's car, in addition to her boyfriend moving in, so tension was high, and the house was crowded.

I moved back in with my mom into her "new to her" smaller single-wide. She had moved and attached our old one room pink addition off the backdoor, converting her place into a three bedroom. That fourteen-foot squared addition was one of the few things she ended up with in the divorce. We acquired it after Terri passed and added it onto the front of our trailer.

I had gotten a job as a hostess at Little America Restaurant in Wyoming, then switched over to being a maid. I was able to ride the Little America employee bus back and forth to work. I was there for a year after graduation while my boyfriend was still in college. I was impatiently waiting for him to finish so we could get married and have a family of our own. All I ever truly longed for was to get married, be a wife, and a mother.

I imagined lots of children to love and have them love me in return.

My boyfriend was in the ROTC program at the University of Wyoming. We would see each other occasionally on weekends and holidays. When we were not together, my mom would try to convince me to break up with him, even resorting to calling one of the counselors from the Orem, Utah, facility we attended prior, begging him to help persuade me; he even showed up at our house to do just that. My boyfriend and I had other ideas. He had come up with a brilliant plan to set us up for our future together. We would get married and join the military; you got paid more in the military if you were married. I would enlist in the US Navy because it was the safest, and after he graduated, he would be a Marine. We would sacrifice four years of our lives in service to our country, save money, and set ourselves up for a long and happy life, our future together. I eagerly agreed as it resulted in what I wanted most. I was sworn into the Navy on Thursday and we were married the next day, Friday, May 29, 1992, at the Uinta County Courthouse. After four days of marriage, I flew out on Tuesday for boot camp.

I had never flown before, and other than one time driving to Texas with my family, I had never been further than Utah. I must have looked as lost as I felt in the large Orlando Florida Airport. Helpers recognized me and shuffled me to the USO conference room which quickly filled up with several recruits. Uniformed men started yelling and lining us up to board buses for transport to the boot camp location. The yelling commenced in the airport and continued for the next two months. My mom yelled at me for years, but this was different. This yelling demanded action and could not be ignored with a retreat to my bedroom or me telling them to "F" off.

I was in an integrated company; some men hated it as they did not join the military to be held back by women. I had not expected them to chop my long locks to my chin, but the recruiter lied. Keep in mind that other than my occasional half-hearted participation in PE and a rare treasure hunt hike, I had never done vigorous physical activity. Soon I was running and marching in newly issued steel-toed boots resulting in blisters, shin splints, and varicose veins. I was doing so many pushups and sit-ups; my abdomen was on fire; I physically could not do one more to save my life. It was hot in Florida, but I did not sweat, I just turned beet red and clammy, my nickname was "No Sweat."

We marched everywhere, to trainings, classes, uniform issue, the barracks, and the mess hall. We quickly got our food, and once the last person at the table sat down, we had fifteen minutes to eat. When the timer went off, you were done, finished or not. I learned to eat everything before the buzzer. We filed in a single line with our undershirt sleeves rolled up as we stepped toward each set of air pressured immunization guns, one for each arm, then stepped to the next, then the next and so on, probably 20-24 shots in total.

During that time, I only received one letter from my husband. Some of the guys couldn't believe he would marry me and send me off to the military. I couldn't believe that I had to go to the bathroom, without stall doors. One girl liked to stand and visit while I was going to the bathroom, I hated it; it was definitely the worst part of the entire experience.

On Sundays, we had the option to clean the barracks or go to church. I took the opportunity to try different churches: Catholic, Southern Baptist, and a few others I can't recall. I went to the Mormon church one time, as that is what I was baptized into when I was eight years old. I no longer believed it though, or that God had a clue what He was doing. I tried them all just to get out of cleaning. They broke us down so they could build us up. I questioned if I had a clue, after they sat us down and informed us that it didn't matter why we joined the military. We were there to DIE for our country if that's what we needed to do.

After successfully graduating from boot camp with my class, I was able to return home for fifteen days before reporting back to "A" school. I visited with my family, planned and carried out our wedding reception, with my mom's help of course. She did not make my dress, but she did make my bouquet and other flowers, the cake, and many of the decorations. We transformed the Lyman church gym into a medieval-themed reception in black and red with an extra-large, cardboard, chalk painted dragon guarding a treasure chest of wedding gifts. It was nice, and several people attended including both sets of grandparents, friends, and other family members. Not everyone that was invited was able to attend, including my dad, although him not showing up was no surprise as we were estranged. Those fifteen days flew by, and before I knew it, I was on a plane headed to San Diego.

My sister and I loved the 80s artists and their music. Some of her favorites were Brian Adams—"Heaven," Phil Collins—"Against All Odds," Van Halen—"Jump," among others. I enjoyed David Lee Roth's song, "California Girls," and I was going to be a California girl. I was stationed in San Diego for five months for Electrical "A" school. On base were several different schools and groups of barracks by each school building. A mess hall for eating, a club for dancing, and a game hall for billiards and darts. The weather was great, not what I was used to being from Wyoming. The base didn't seem that far from the beach for swimming and sunbathing, or the outdoor malls for shopping. To the south of my building was another similar building. It was loosely wrapped in plastic as it was being carefully disassembled due to the asbestos. I walked back and forth in front of that building several times a day for five months to get to my classroom. I was exposed to a lot of different people and new ideas on that base.

Just to the east of my multi-level barracks was an empty identical structure. One day, the officers assembled all the inhabitants of my building outside for an announcement. We were informed that male sailors had been sneaking into the empty building to watch the girls with east facing windows get dressed. We were instructed to be cautious and keep our curtains closed while dressing. After the public announcement to the entire building, my roommate and I were pulled aside and informed that they were sneaking in there to watch me. We were given permission to have contraband clips to close the four-inch gap that existed even when the curtains were completely closed. We were assured that we would not get in trouble for them during our room inspections. I sobbed, felt embarrassed and emotionally violated. I didn't want people to think I was pretty. I just wanted everyone to leave me alone. To this day I still hate the feeling that I am being watched.

My husband and I didn't talk much, but when we did, it always included arguing and him asking if I had sent him money and whether or not I had cheated on him yet. For months, my answers were always yes, I have sent the money, and no, I have not cheated on you. These conversations would take place on one of the payphones by my barracks and was never as private as I would have liked. Several concerned male friends would advise me on my struggling marriage, if you could call it a marriage. I heeded their helpful advice and reasoned with my eighteen-year-old self that, if I was already receiving the punishment, I may as well commit the crime. I stopped sending him money, and finally one day when he asked if I had cheated on him, my answer was not no. Cheating was expected of me, so I decided just to get it out of the way, although I had to get drunk to do it. While at the club drinking and dancing, I stumbled outside with a guy. We didn't get far from the club; being a good dancer did not equate to being good at the other stuff. I didn't realize until after that we were by a large dumpster, which was very fitting, because I was trash!

When my husband asked me if I had cheated and my answer was yes, the phone went quiet for what seemed like forever, then I asked him what he intended to do.

He replied, "Get a divorce, I guess?"

I said "okay" and gave up so easily.

After ending that conversation, I immediately called my mom. She happened to be at my grandma and grandpa's house in Vernal. I told her that I was getting a divorce and what I had done to cause it. I had her pass the phone around to all present family members so I could be the one to tell them firsthand. When I spoke with one of my aunts, she told me not to feel too bad because he had been cheating on me for quite some time. That revelation led me down an eye-opening path, our long-distance marriage never had a chance. Our divorce was great. While home on leave, we spent a week as husband and wife, then drove to the courthouse together, signed and filed the papers, ending our eight-month marriage and our four-year relationship. Our plan, our brilliant plan of being together forever did not work.

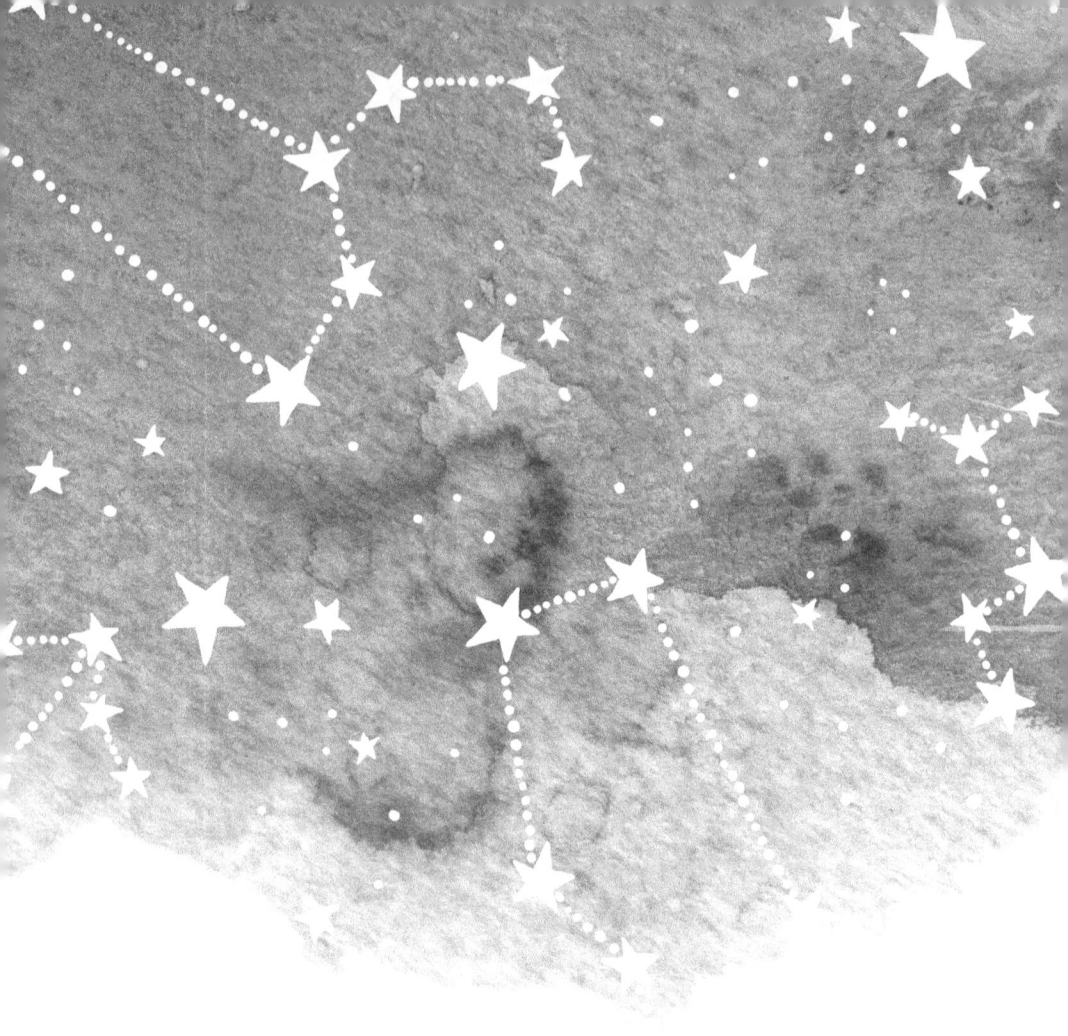

Ex·pres·sion

The process of making known one's thoughts or feelings.

CHAPTER SIX

Riotous Living

*E*VEN THOUGH I mostly hated kindergarten through twelfth grade, I actually did very well with my electrical training in the Navy. I understood it and liked hands-on learning. I ended up finishing at the top of my class. As a result of doing well in "A" school, I was sent to "C" school. After each, I was able to go back home on leave. My time was not well spent. When I was not getting divorced, I partied and made one bad decision after the other. Alcohol was always involved; although, it was a pathetic excuse for my behavior, I would not have been able to do all the things I was doing without it, it helped me stay desensitized.

I continued in that unfeeling state while in Norfolk, Virginia, for my four weeks of "C" school where I was trained to troubleshoot, maintain, and repair the PT 512 Tactical Display Plotting System. The plotter was a big table with a glass top. It was designed to generate a large map showing the ship's position in relation to friendly and enemy forces. It provided a picture of the battlefield so important tactical decisions could be made. The irony was lost on me at the time—I could repair a nautical navigational device that could detect potential hazards. Yet, I had no idea what I was doing, where I was going, or that I was surrounded by danger. At the time I would have lit up as the biggest enemy to myself.

Education was the one thing that I had going for me. My personal life was in shambles, and I was self-destructive. I was off course, alone, scared, angry, and I had no idea the damage I was doing. People sucked, men sucked, love hurt, and pain was real. I didn't want to feel it, so I stayed numb. I continued to fall deeper into despair and darkness, I felt nothing positive there. I committed to not being a victim so I would put my guard up and cause pain to others before they had a chance to hurt me. I was hard-hearted and sometimes brutal. I spent a year or so playing tug-of-war with myself, and my feelings, trying to keep people out emotionally but having minimal boundaries physically. I hated myself. I was hit on by men and women and admitted that I was attracted to both. Never having defined rules in that area allowed for exploration. I explored a lot of things. I was trying to figure out life but was searching for answers in all the wrong places. I was introduced to the Ouija board and consulted it a couple of times. I was skeptical the first time, and the second time my dead sister told me not to mess with it anymore. I never touched it again. I was cynical and untrusting. Tarot cards turned into a fancy horoscope reading. Advice from others was not fitting for my situation. Guys wanted to sweep me off my feet, sleep with me, and or marry me, but I just wanted to dance.

I left Norfolk, went on leave, then returned to San Diego. I was assigned to the USS *Acadia* (AD 42). It was a destroyer tender. It was an integrated ship and was nicknamed the "love boat." When I got to the vessel, I was required to serve a couple of months on mess duty before starting my electrical assignment. It was not bad. Me and another gal helped serve, stock and refill all the drinks and food as we worked the beverage line and salad bar. It was a good introduction to the environment and the people. Although I was stationed on the boat, while docked, we could leave after work. Again, I went to the beach, shopping, out to eat; Rice King was my favorite. I went to the movies, hotels, parties, and to several different clubs on base, in San Diego, and Tijuana, dancing. I would often stay out clubbing until three or four in the morning then go back to the ship, shower, lay in my rack for an hour or so, get up at five a.m., throw on my uniform, and start all over again.

I finished that assignment and began working as an Interior Communications Electrician, which is what I went to school for. While docked, we worked from seven to four. We were assigned to rotating guard duty once every six days and would have different assignments; on those days we could not leave the ship. During working hours, we removed and installed equipment, electrical cables, flood alarms, and routinely checked all electrical devices throughout the ship, plus more. I grew a backbone and learned to stick up for myself, mostly. I was later moved to the "tool shed" after reporting some sexual misconduct from a fellow sailor. In the summer of 1993, we started practicing fire drills and battle trials in preparation for our pending six-month deployment we referred to as, "WestPac."

In early November we left California and headed to our first stop, Hawaii. The ocean was rough, and I was surprised how much the boat swayed and how seasick I became, but it got better, or maybe I got used to it. I was looking forward to having a better time in Hawaii for this trip, as my last one turned out to be another negative experience. I had flown over to spend some of my leave time with a guy I had hooked up with several times and showed hints of a relationship. After his time in California, he was stationed in Hawaii and invited me to come spend time with him. Once I arrived, he was happy to see me but soon started to get rough with me. Later, we had a physical altercation; he hit, pushed, shoved, and knocked me around a bit. I gathered my belongings and spent the night in a nearby concrete and cinder block public restroom. I had nowhere to go, no one to help me. As I sat crying on the cold hard floor, I leaned against the trash can and once again pondered how my trip was a waste and how my life and I were both garbage; God did make junk, I was proof. I changed my flight and went back to California early and never discussed my disappointing trip.

Hawaii was better the second time. I rented an electric scooter and did some sightseeing. I don't know the name of the beach, but the ocean seemed more powerful there. I waded out into the salty water to swim and splash around. When I decided to go back to shore, I could not get out of the water. It kept pulling me down, thrashing me around, and burying me under the sand over and over with every powerful wave. I was terrified, and pretty sure I was going to die.

Finally, after fighting for what seemed like forever, I was able to escape the massive Pacific. I was covered in sand in places I didn't even know I had. I decided that the ocean was cruel, like life, and I didn't like it.

Next, we made a brief stop in Guam. We went shopping for supplies and had a short group outing jumping off the wooden docks and playing in the water. Hong Kong was next with more shopping and clubbing. I would send my mom various souvenirs like oriental dolls or china tea sets, my grandma Sue always got collector spoons. I never heard from my dad or anyone on that side of my family.

Our vessel was unexpectedly rerouted and ended up off the coast of Mogadishu with hostile gunfire ashore. We had to keep the ship dark and could not go above deck. We were there for support, repairs, and supplies. Some of us carried parts from our boat over to the US *Kitty Hawk*, out in the middle of the ocean. I scrambled down the ladder of our watercraft and carefully climbed into a yellow rubber raft. The waves thrashed us around as we made our way to the aircraft carrier where we scurried up the ladder into one of the decks. I got to tour the *Kitty Hawk*, exchange parts, acquire their logoed ball cap, and visit with fellow sailors. I was equally shocked and impressed with that floating city. The approximately five thousand plus crew members more than doubled the population of my hometown.

I spent a lonely Christmas out on the Pacific Ocean that year. My mom made me a handcrafted, twelve-inch, fabric Christmas tree with battery lights. She lovingly made sequined beaded felt ornaments that velcroed on in advent calendar fashion, homemade cookies, and a batch of caramels. Although she sent it in plenty of time, receiving mail was inefficient at best. The cookies were a bag of crumbs by the time I received them, but they were the best crumbs ever, and my carefully cut caramels were in one large clump that my friends and I were happy to rip bites off until it was devoured. Those gifts were a small taste of home and helped me make it through the unorthodox holidays.

My memory is a bit blurry to the exact chronological order of the trip, but my experiences and feelings are very clear. Visiting Bali was one of my favorites. It was beautiful there with shopping, clubbing, and sightseeing. The lush green trees, scenery, and several life-sized marble sculptures were exquisite. I enjoyed the comfort of the motel with all the rooms lined in a rectangle, framing a large swimming pool. It was a nice break from my two-and-a-half by six-and-a-half-foot top bunk.

Early one morning, I was ripped out of that same bunk to start the long day of initiation that was inflicted upon all of the newbies. It was a tradition for all who wanted to participate, although I knew a girl who chose not to, and I think her punishment lasted much longer than just the one day. The crew members that had previously crossed the equator spent weeks in preparation stiffening their firehose paddles in salt water and stockpiling the garbage. If you had never crossed the equator, you were on the receiving end of their excitement. It was not completely terrible. Our clothes were inside out, we were yelled at, pushed around, made to crawl through garbage while lined with onlookers and active paddlers yelling and cheering. We were hosed down at close range with a firehose of forceful salty seawater that stung as it pelted my body and burned my eyes. In the end, we were accepted as part of an exclusive group of sailors that had traveled the world crossing the imaginary line drawn around the center of the earth.

By the time we got to Saudi Arabia, I had a boyfriend of sorts. We started hanging out as friends, and he planted a few seeds—one being that I needed to improve my behavior, and the other was that I was living beneath myself. It was casual and easy. I didn't have the energy to put into other people, I needed it for myself just to get through. I was barely staying afloat. He did not expect a relationship or marriage because he was already in one he was trying to get out of, he said it was pretty bad. He was safe for me, we hung out on and off the ship, we had fun. He was approached by a Saudi Arabian man who offered to pay me ten thousand dollars if I would have sex with him. Men there did not speak directly to women; in his chivalry, he turned it down and told me about it later. He was easy on the eyes and the ears, as he could sing. I would go admire him practicing with his alternative rock band down in the lower decks of the ship. I let my guard down with him, I softened, we became intimate, and I fell for him even though I knew we would never be together.

He was not the only singer I was able to enjoy listening to overseas. I attended a concert in Hong Kong. I cleared a path for myself to the front of the large industrial building, all the way up to the stage, where Brian Adams reached out and grabbed my hand. I was reminded of how much I missed my sister as he sang "Heaven." While there, I tested and received a Hong Kong driver's license, on my first try. I was able to legally drive on the wrong side of the road. I would travel from dock to dock in a small jeep, almost golf cart size, delivering parts to other ships. It was very crowded there; so many people, yet I still managed to feel alone. They had oversized glass walled malls for shopping, clubs for dancing, and fancy hotels for the other stuff. I made permanent reminders and lasting memories in Hong Kong, including a self-drawn tattoo, and oh, I took one other thing with me.

Prior to setting course back home, more ports were scheduled: Sasebo and Yokosuka Japan. The ship was sailing to Guam, then Hawaii again before arriving back in San Diego in mid-April 1994. Although that was the ship's plan, my plans changed. While in Sasebo, Japan, I learned that I was expecting. I called my mom from a payphone booth to share my exciting news with her. I could not remain on the ship in my condition and was flown out of Sasebo on a fifteen-hour flight back to San Diego with new orders. I had been appointed to the base on Coronado Bay. It was an island just off the coast of San Diego accessible by water, or the two-mile bridge. I had no established credit, but with the help and willingness of my grandma Sue's co-signature, I was able to purchase my dark, sparkly, hunter green Nissan sedan and would drive over that bridge.

I moved over into an available room shortly after receiving my orders as a mailroom custodian, with security clearance. The building was similar to a multi-level apartment building with each floor having a living room and kitchenette shared by eight females. Two girls in each of the four private beds and bathrooms that branched off the common room. Late one morning alone in my room, I awoke to my higher-ranking supervisor sitting beside me on my bed. He had quietly let himself into my room to check on me after I had called off due to morning sickness. He proposed to me and offered me a life with him in one home, with two master bedrooms and another couple. We could all share, have my baby and many others, creating a large happy family. I shockingly declined and was encouraged to turn him in for sexual harassment, as he was inappropriate and made going to work very uncomfortable. This time the guy was relocated, not me.

As it got closer to my due date, I was reassigned back over to the San Diego base. I was able to get into off-base military housing. It was a two-bedroom apartment, with a twenty-min-ute drive to work. One of the other expecting single mothers from another room on the same floor of my apartment moved in across the street from me. I started nesting and was able to buy furniture; a black pleather couch and loveseat, and a

Whirlpool washer and dryer. I purchased a used crib, clothes, and needed items to prepare for my baby's arrival. Before I knew the gender of the baby, I bought a tiny pair of work boots. I didn't care if it was a boy or a girl, but I thought I might be more suited to raising a boy. My new "friend" across the street, we will call her Jill, was having a boy. However, she was undecided as to whether or not she would keep him.

Jill and I were very different. I had always wanted children, like ten or twelve of them. She didn't want any and even contemplated terminating her pregnancy. She decided against it and as an alternative was considering adoption. I grew up around plenty of babies, being one of the older cousins I helped with them all the time. Jill had no experience with infants or children. We both learned that if we stayed on active duty, we would be required to sign over guardianship of our children to someone who could care for and raise them if we were to get deployed. She had no one, I had my mom but hated the idea of not being with my own child. I had an aunt and uncle offer to adopt my baby, if I chose to go that route, but it never crossed my mind. I decided to fill out papers requesting an early discharge from the military as they were offering to release service members from their contracts at that time under a reduction in force initiative.

I helped Jill prepare for her delivery. We shared our experiences growing up and things we had been through. The life she was familiar with scared me. I learned how her mother was not in her life, and she did not believe in God. She was raised without religion and left to fend for herself; she was truly alone. She explained how she was into crystals, tarot cards, Ouija boards, devil worshiping, and spirit swapping. She was involved in performing satanic rituals, one that had specifically

DESIRES OF A PRODIGAL DAUGHTER

resulted in a pentagram bewitchingly scratched into the carpet and filled with blood. She had a relationship with a celebrity, after a ritual transferred his spirit into her female friend's body, and they dated for three years. I was surprised and concerned that she found all that normal. When I was in her apartment on a few occasions, I could literally feel evil breathing down the back of my neck.

I told her, "You know you're not alone in here, right?"

She replied that she was aware and that, "ALL spirits were welcome."

Those same dark spirits would follow me home, but I had been recently taught at church that I could command evil spirits to depart through the power of the priesthood, they were not allowed in my house.

Jill was due about a month before me. My mother had come to stay with and assist me, and both of us accompanied Jill in the delivery room so she would not be alone, and I would gain firsthand knowledge about what I was soon going to experience. After her baby boy was born, she still was not certain what she should do, and I never learned what happened to her or what was decided. I just knew that she lacked hope as I once did.

Sister Runia summed up my thoughts perfectly when she said, "Satan, the great accuser and deceiver, uses shame to keep us from God. Shame is a darkness so heavy it feels that if you took it out of your body, it would have an actual weight or heft to it. Shame is the voice that beats you up, saying, 'What were you thinking?' 'Do you ever get anything right?' Shame doesn't tell us we made a mistake; it tells us we are our mistakes. You may even hear, 'Hide.' The adversary does everything in his power to keep the heaviness inside, telling us the cost is too high,

that it will be easier if this stays in darkness, removing all hope."
~ *Tamara W. Runia, first counselor in the Young Women's Presidency of The Church of Jesus Christ of Latter-day Saints.*

Satan had convinced me his lies were true, and those inaccurate beliefs kept me weighed down, in dark despair for many years. I knew I could not offer hope to my child or to others if I did not have it for myself.

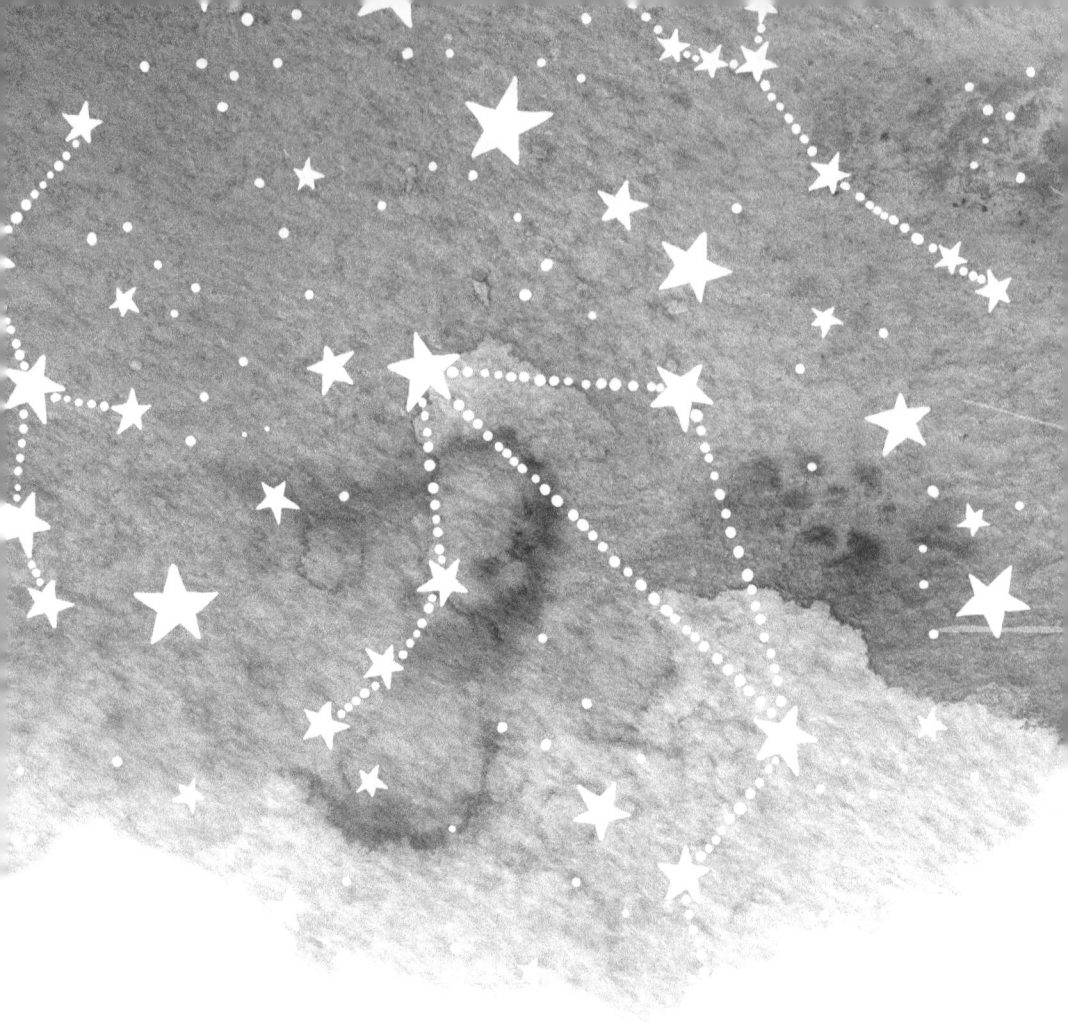

Re·birth

A spiritual enlightenment
causing a person to lead
a new life.

CHAPTER SEVEN

Coming to Myself

WHEN I FOUND OUT I was pregnant, I was so excited. I had always wanted a baby to love and love me back. However, I started to ponder if I was good enough to be a mother, and I concluded that in my current condition, I was not. I knew I wasn't on the right path and that road did not lead me where I desired to go in life. I wanted better for myself and especially my child. I knew that I had made multiple bad decisions, and I didn't think I could undo all the things that I had done, but I wanted to try. I desired to do better, be better. I had pushed God away a long time ago, after my sister died. I didn't know Him well enough to trust Him. I was born into the gospel but not raised in the gospel. I didn't know if it was true or just a ruse that parents use to guilt their children into obedience. I took scriptures with me on the ship, a Bible and a Book of Mormon. I rarely touched them other than to move them aside in my locker to get to other things. My baby's biological father got me thinking that I needed to improve, but the reality of a baby moved up my timeline. On my own, I didn't know where to start.

There I was out in the middle of the ocean, alone. I had never felt so lonely, insignificant, or hopeless standing on the top deck surrounded by nothing but deep navy blue for as far as the eye could see, darkness in every direction. I contemplated my place in the universe and wondered if God really existed. I understood why early explorers thought the earth was flat. There is a hard line between the water and the sky. It looked like we were going to get to the edge and fall off, but as the ship kept inching forward, so did that edge. I desired to see past the illusion, beyond what I could comprehend with my mortal sight. Even though I was scared, I moved toward it, toward God into the unknown. My mind caught hold of Jesus, and I cried out to God with my whole soul. I confessed that I had no idea what I was doing and begged Him for His help; *I surrendered*. In that exact moment, like the prodigal son, I was succored and wrapped in Heavenly Father's robe, encircled with warmth, peace, and love, almost like a hug. The stars came into view, brightened the horizon, and illuminated the sky.

For the first time in years, I could see light and feel hope.

Reaching out to God was just the first step. I had lots of work to do. I decided that I would go back to church, not really knowing if The Church of Jesus Christ of Latter-day Saints was true, but I resolved that I would start there and figure it out along the way. It helped that once back in California, one of my sister's best friend's husband was stationed there. Susan lived about thirty minutes away from my military housing, and I would spend time with her and her kids, attend church with them, and stay for Sunday dinners. I watched my first General Conference with her. I can't recall how we even connected, but she was a Godsend; I'm not sure if I would have stayed active without her. I worked with the bishop, confessed and forsook my sins. As part of my repentance process, I did not partake of the sacrament ordinance for a while, it almost seemed too easy.

Susan's young daughter noticed one Sunday that I had not taken the sacrament and very loudly asked why I did not eat a piece of bread. I was embarrassed, but the issue was quickly resolved without an in-depth discussion. I was not capable of explaining, nor did I fully comprehend the details of going through the beautiful repentance process. At that time, it was painful, I had not arrived at the beautiful part yet.

I was able to go back home for some much-needed leave before I had my baby and could still travel. My family on my mom's side missed me and were excited to see me. By then I learned I was having a girl, and of course, everyone wanted to know what I was going to name her. I had put a lot of thought into finding a unique name. I decided to name her Saxen, her middle name, Sue, after my mom and Grandma and her last name, my maiden name, same as me. Some of my leave was spent in Vernal where both Grandma and Grandpa Mac, Mom, and I made a baby quilt together. The fabric was white with a pink bow print. We tied it with pink satin ribbon and trimmed it with white lace. I felt my family's love and support for me, and I hoped more than anything that Saxen would always know and feel how much she was loved as well.

During my pregnancy, I experienced great stress and anxiety. I was trying to get out of the military, get my life on track, and figure out what my next move should be. As I kept trudging forward as an infant in the gospel and a first-time mother, my mom came out to California to live with me. She brought my brother with her, but he didn't stay very long. Mom never remarried after she and my dad divorced, so she was able to uproot her life and come help me with mine. I appreciated her and her willingness to do so.

I started having contractions, but as soon as they laid me down in the hospital, progress stopped. They sent me to go walk around, so we did, then everything started again and back to the Naval Hospital we went. Both Susan and Mom were in the delivery room when my daughter was born—I was in labor forever.

The doctor and several trainees would all come in and fill the room to check my progress. I received an epidural that eventually wore off. They had placed a catheter and prepared me for a c-section. However, the hospital got busy, and they left me unattended for too long. The baby moved into the birth canal and started pushing on the catheter. I was dilated to a ten and actively pushed for eight hours prior to the delivery. They used forceps, and I ended up tearing all the way through, as a result I required over one hundred and twenty running stitches.

I had hoped that I would have had Saxen on my dad's birthday, but God had other plans. She was born early in the morning on December 8, 1994. During delivery, she had a heart attack and was born under much distress. She had a floppy heart valve and a small clot and was admitted to the ICU.

Saxen looked so out of place there as most of the babies in ICU were premature and underdeveloped. She was full term, weighed nine pounds, four ounces, and was nineteen inches long. She filled the entire clear plastic infant bed. With everything she had going on, I requested that she be given a priesthood blessing. Saxen was blessed with healing and a quick recovery. The doctors were astonished that her clot dissolved and her floppy valve corrected itself. I know the reason she was only in the ICU for a week is because we received a miracle. I was also blessed being a single mother with military benefits, that the entire ordeal for both of us ended up costing me only sixty-eight dollars out of pocket—another miracle.

Saxen's biological father came to see her in the hospital as well as my dad. Both short visits, but some effort was there. I was given some maternity leave and did not have to return to work for a while. Mom and I finally went home to my apartment and introduced Saxen to her new home. Mom sewed her a handmade baby blue dress trimmed in eyelet lace and country blue ribbon with a matching diaper cover. I did not want Saxen to be too "girly." Mom also crocheted her an afghan in pastels and sewed a matching crib set. It was white with baby footprints in delicate shades of color. I cut out hands and feet from a roll of subtle floral contact paper to temporarily decorate the walls.

Saxen was a very fussy baby; she would not take a binky and needed hours of rocking and consoling. I was exhausted. Mom was a huge relief. We prepared for the holidays, set up a tree, and went to a movie on Christmas Eve at the movie theater.

As a Christmas gift, another friend of mine gave Saxen a pair of tiny diamond earrings for her soon-to-be pierced ears. I intended on having her ears pierced at the three-month mark, as soon as they would let me get them done.

When I was younger, I wanted my ears pierced and begged my mom for months. Finally, she gave in. We were in Vernal, and at eight years old, I sat so big in the chair. The loud painful gun pierced one ear, and I flew out of the chair, out the door, and halfway down the block. They had to drag me back in to finish the second ear. Then when I was fourteen, I decided that I wanted two holes in each ear and was going to do it myself.

I numbed my left ear with ice; gave an extended painful effort to push the needle through the crunchy layers of my earlobe. After one was finished, I decided that was good enough. I did not need two holes in my right ear; time did not make me tougher in that department.

I figured that my daughter would want her ears pierced, so I decided to skip the begging; painful experience and just get them done while still young enough not to remember.

I was overwhelmed as a parent and all that I needed to decide for my child. My daughter was at the mercy of an inexperienced mother, a struggling adult, a broken human being, and a newly discovered daughter of God trying to improve and figure out her own life. All those years of babysitting did not prepare me for twenty-four-seven parenting. I thought I knew a lot about kids, and still I was in over my head. My daughter had no idea that she would be raising me. It was a good thing I bought her those work boots, because I was going to be a lot of work.

My ex-husband and I had been exchanging letters for a few months. He had gotten word that I was expecting a baby and had questions about the details. It pushed some buttons for the both of us, as having children together was part of our long-term plan. It was just another reminder that life had not turned out how we expected. He came to San Diego to visit after Saxen was born and offered to assist; he wanted to marry me again and be a family. He assured me that it would be different, and he would love my daughter as his own.

As tempting as that suggestion was, I wanted more. Not only did I not want to parent alone, but I also did not want to live the gospel alone either. I desired it in my life, for my family, and I wanted a husband who would live it with me. He was unwilling to make that commitment. I declined his proposition as gently and firmly as I knew how. I never stopped loving him, but I had always loved him, and I knew that love was not enough. It broke my heart all over again.

Through it all, I kept going to church, paying my tithing, and working with the bishop. Before leaving San Diego, I received my patriarchal blessing, Mom was with me. That individualized blessing comes through inspiration, via a Patriarch; it provides lineage, promises, gifts, admonitions, and direction. I had never met the Patriarch before that day; I felt the Spirit strongly during my blessing, and I knew it came from God. That conduit was not aware that my sister had passed away. However, as a magnificent tender mercy, I was blessed to know that it was Terri's time and God's plan for her, as she had a special mission in heaven. My blessing helped me continue to heal, forgive, understand, and more deeply feel God's love for me.

CHAPTER EIGHT

Born Again

I WAS NOT QUITE READY to move back home, so Saxen and I stayed a week with my cousin in Texas. By the middle of April, we were back in my hometown and living with my mother. She had purchased a lot in the privately owned section of the trailer park and moved her little single-wide on it. The two-bedroom, one bath with our pink addition attached off the back door, and we were relocated once again. The front room had mauve carpet that matched her black oriental sectional with mauve and turquoise that looked like paint wisps. She drove my car to her job during the day while I stayed home with Saxen. I was receiving a hundred dollars a month disability from the military, some child support, and working a graveyard shift while Mom stayed home with my daughter.

Her working days and me working nights functioned well for us. I continued to work with my local stake president in order to acquire a desired recommend necessary for attending the temple. After lots of effort, repentance, a few setbacks, and some temple prep classes, I was finally able to obtain my recommend and receive the temple endowment for myself. As I had been forewarned, it was a bit odd and overwhelming at first. One definitely needs to continue going to discover the symbolism and mysteries that can only be unfolded in the house of God. Our ways are not His ways; His are more glorious and beautiful.

My brother and his wife were living in Provo, Utah, at this time, and my sister-in-law was working at an Arby's. They set me up on a blind date with the franchise owner's son who was her boss. They owned several locations, and he was managing that restaurant. Their son was a returned missionary and still single. He had graduated from BYU, sang, played the piano, was kind, and came from a good active family. He was aware of my situation and was willing to overlook my past, to love, forgive, and marry me in the temple. We had a short courtship, and he proposed while sitting on the couches in the celestial room of the Jordan River Temple of The Church of Jesus Christ of Latter-day Saints.

Although I was not in love with him, I agreed. I had received advice that I could learn to love him in time, and that I may not get another opportunity given my history. I was reassured that he checked all of the important boxes that the church tells you to look for and are ideal to have. We were sealed in the temple as an eternal family. My aspirations were finally coming true.

We had to secure permission from Saxen's biological father in order to have her sealed to us, which he willingly provided. Although I had very few active members in my family and they could not go inside, many still came to support me, including my dad. We had a nice luncheon afterward and a reception the next day. My new husband performed a musical number; he played the piano and sang to me. The experience checked all of the boxes I had in my head, and we looked the part. I had expectations of what a temple marriage should look like.

I thought that living the gospel as a couple and as a family came with an understanding that we were going to uphold gospel principles, go to church, pray, read together, have family home evening, attend the temple, pay tithing, and that my husband would use and share his priesthood to bless our family. In addition to what we should be doing, I also expected that there were certain things we would not do.

My dreams of an ideal temple marriage shortly turned into a nightmare. I learned that spouses cannot hide their true feelings or cravings for very long. I did not feel that my daughter and I were safe, and I was not going to stick around for something worse to happen. I asked why he was not honest with me about his gospel standards and other issues.

He told me, "I thought if I had, you wouldn't have married me."

"You're damn right, I wouldn't have married you, and I'm not going to stay." After only five months of marriage, I escaped, although not entirely—I was expecting another baby.

I went to the bishop and requested a temple divorce; however, it was not granted. It was explained to me that although we would not be together as husband and wife, keeping the sealing ordinance in place tied me to my children and all of us to God. Important eternal blessings and promises were still in force. I did not understand how it all worked, but I was assured that God would manage the details, and I trusted that He would.

Once again divorced, pregnant, crushed, and heart broken, I was back in Lyman living with my mother. And again, I was confused and angry with God. The first time I did everything wrong; I did what I wanted without asking for God's help. I was a mess, and my life turned out to be a mess. The second time,

I thought I had done everything right; what I was expected to do, what everyone told me I was supposed to do as a member of the church.

I definitely learned that getting married in the temple and having a covenant keeping, committed marriage are two completely different things. I didn't want a life that looked good on the outside, I wanted a life that was actually good. I thought that's what I was getting. I was praying and asking for help, and it still turned out to be a mess. I was at a loss; I didn't know what to do. Maybe I was junk, perhaps I was not lovable or deserving of a good life? I was back at square one. I thought I had figured a few things out, but apparently, I knew nothing, I still had no idea what I was doing.

Janice was a friend from high school. She and her fiancé Lance bought a house next to my mom and were living kitty-corner across the street from us. I was invited to their wedding. Her soon-to-be husband was not only my cousin, but he was also my sister's age, and he hung out with her, some, when she was alive. Many of his friends that would be in attendance were my sister's attractive, dreamy classmates. It was a reminder that my sister would never get married or have a family of her own. With everything I was going through, I did not want any of them to see me or talk to me. I felt I was a failure, and I was embarrassed. I made it a point to go to Utah on their wedding day and "did not make it back in time." That was my lame excuse as I did not have the strength to attend or explain.

We still remained friends, and when it was time for my son to be born, Janice, now expecting herself, accompanied my mom and me to the hospital in Provo. I was actively in labor until they laid me down and got everything hooked up, then labor stopped; the same thing that happened with my first baby. It was late when they sent us home, so we stayed at my cousin's apartment close by. He and his wife were going to school in Provo, but that night they were out of town and offered it to us so we were able to get a good night's sleep.

The next morning when I was getting dressed to go back home, I expressed my frustration and asked out loud, "Am I ever going to have this baby?" As soon as I asked, my baby answered; he kicked me and my water broke. It was assured that Skyler would arrive, and we would not need to make a second trip. I had learned after my first child that as soon as you get to the hospital, it takes forever, and they won't let you eat. I insisted we go to breakfast before I went to have my son.

I was calm upon arrival and informed the nurse that I was in labor, again. She questioned how I knew; I stepped back from the counter and gestured to my third pair of wet pants. Nurses scurried to get me set up in my room. Some were lacking in bedside manner, and my mom pulled one off to the side for what I can assume was a scolding because they were nicer to me after her conversation with them. Things moved along much faster than with my first child. My same friend, Susan, who lived in California and was in the delivery room with me there, was now living in Provo and made it just in time to be in the room with me for my second child's birth also, joining my mom and Janice. After being fully dilated, I pushed three times, and he was born, weighing nine pounds, two ounces. I was surprised and commented, "That's it? I could do that again."

Two children with two entirely different experiences. Not only were the birthing experiences night and day but so were my children. Skyler was a wonderful baby; he was content and seldom cried, unlike Saxen. He was her baby too. She adored him and helped feed, burp, change, and dress him. The love she had for her brother was the sweetest thing to watch.

It took well over a year to finalize my divorce; along with being pregnant, I was lonely. I had my daughter, then my son, a few family members, some friends, and my mother. But those relationships were not the same as a partner. Although I was grateful for them, I yearned for a complete family of my own. I went on a few dates but nothing promising.

Across the street, Lance and Janice were building a garage, and one of the construction workers had noticed me a few times and inquired about me. Although Janice warned me and tried to deter him, he was their friend and kept encouraging her to set something up. I knew this guy from high school; when he was a senior, he was short and looked like he was twelve years old. Back then, I thought he was a cocky jerk, and I didn't like him. I drug my feet a bit but agreed to call him. We talked a few times and eventually ended up on a double date with our mutual friends.

We went to the Lyman theater and watched the newly released movie *Liar, Liar*, with Jim Carrey. I was told, but still pleasantly surprised, that Scott had gotten taller and no longer looked twelve, he was actually quite attractive. We were both nervous, and he was slow and strategic about holding my hand. The movie was hilarious, we all laughed and enjoyed it. Afterward, we hung out at Lance and Janice's for a bit, then he walked me home. He tried to kiss me goodnight on the front porch, but I turned my head, and he kissed my cheek. He awkwardly left and lightly jogged down the steps and back across the street. I witnessed his skillful recovery when he stepped off the sidewalk into a dip almost twisting his ankle. I quietly giggled as I watched him and was also aware that my brother and sister-in-law had been peeking through the window the entire time.

We kept talking and decided to go out on another date, but he stood me up the second time. I informed him I was not into being jerked around. That as a single mom, I didn't have time for it. He apologized, and we went out several more times. I enjoyed hanging out with him, but he was not someone that looked very good on paper—though, better than me if someone tallied my situation.

However, after only two short weeks, I felt the strongest burning of the bosom; I knew with every fiber of my being that he was the one. I had never in my life experienced anything like it, but it didn't make any sense to me. Using my own logic, I did not understand why Scott was Mr. Right.

Janice advised me not to be the first one to say, "I love you." I heeded her advice. After about a month of dating, he was as dumb founded as I was. He was looking to have a good time and get out like the others before me. He did not anticipate falling in love with me and my two children.

CHAPTER NINE

Starting Over

I KNOW IT WAS NOT the best excuse, but I had had enough bad sexual experiences and abuse that I could not be with someone without knowing what that part of our relationship was going to look like. I needed to know that I was going to be safe, and that he did not have weird issues or fetishes he was going to surprise me with later. We started seeing each other at the end of June, and he proposed to me the night of my grandparent's fiftieth wedding anniversary celebration on August 2, 1997. After their party, we got the kids to my mom who watched them for us.

Unbeknownst to me, he took me out to the steel bridge, and we climbed on top and straddled the right arch. We sat face-to-face. After visiting for a bit, he pulled out a dime machine adjustable snowman ring and asked me to marry him. Of course, I said yes, we kissed and sat in awe of us and a meteor shower that was lighting up the sky above, while simultaneously admiring its reflection sparkling in the water below.

The next day we drove to Utah and picked out a beautiful trillion cut diamond ring. He spent all of his money he had saved up for hunting on it. On the way, we discussed how his friends had advised him to just live with me and not get married, but he was confident that was an unnecessary step. We shared all of the vital deal-breaking kind of information with each other so we could enter into our marriage without being trapped or tricked. It was scary, but neither of us were deterred by the truth. It was a huge relief not keeping secrets. It was important for me to tell and hear the facts even if I might lose him. It was better to know all the things so we could both make an informed decision, move forward together, and leave the past behind us.

Scott's parents, Allen and Jane, were stunned when we came home and showed them the ring. After four years of playing college basketball, he moved back home and worked construction. He was twenty-six years old, partying and living in their basement. He had managed to avoid settling down and was now engaged to a twice divorced woman with two children. I am sure they were quietly concerned about him and us, especially given our histories and the short timeline. His dad knew right away that he was completely in love with me when he learned that Scott spent his "hunting" money on the ring. It was several weeks later when his mom knew for herself how much he loved me.

I had been having severe abdominal issues. I went to the emergency room, and they sent me home saying it was constipation. However, that "constipation" landed me back in the ER days later. I was in excruciating pain that had me doubled over, weak, and at the edge of consciousness. This time they did blood work and discovered that I had internal bleeding. I was rushed into emergency surgery where they found a ruptured ectopic pregnancy; we had no idea until that very moment. The doctor said a cyst could do the same thing with the same result, so that is the story we told everyone. Regardless, I was left with a six-inch scar across my lower abdomen, one fallopian tube, and my chances of getting pregnant cut in half. Scott absolutely hated hospitals, but he sat by my side for two days. That's when his mom knew, "Scott does not go to hospitals or sit still for anyone." Jane admitted, "He must really love you."

The brutal pain I was in, slowly bleeding internally, later made me ponder what kind of pain my sister must have experienced when she died. I had a hard time believing that she would have laid still in that gutter, just twenty feet off the road, and would not have made her way to get help in the approximately forty-five minutes she agonized and was dying. I uncomfortably thrashed around, unable to hold still in my thirty-minute car ride to the Evanston Hospital. I assumed she would have been able to make it to the busy truck stop, or at least close enough for a driver to see her. Just one more reason I will always wonder.

Scott and I planned to be married after hunting season, of course. He worked and hunted, and I healed, planned, and prepared for the wedding. Mom helped with everything, using her gifts and talents in the wedding-floral department. Everything fell into place. I found my dress and lots of needed items on sale. It seemed to all work out. I helped decorate and made the cake. We were married in our high school gym at center court with a basketball on either side of the backdrop. Basketball had played such a pivotal role in Scott's life, that is where he wanted us to get married.

I entered the ceremony to the song, "Let's Get Ready to Rumble," playing over the loudspeaker. The music changed as my dad continued to walk me down the aisle. Even though I had been married twice before, that was the first time my dad gave me away. We had a rocky relationship, although it was slightly improving, I desired a better one, but it was what it was.

My father-in-law was a bishop, and he had the privilege of marrying us. He had been friends with my grandpa Clinton for many years and joked during our nuptials about Scott marrying into the "Walker" family. Scott was nervous and jittery, although sober, which was a step up from our rehearsal practice.

Scott said, "Sure," instead of, "I do." He thought he was being funny. Allen recovered quickly with a comment that Scott's answer was still in the affirmative. My uncle took our wedding photos, and he videoed advice from our guests. Lance and Janice wished us luck on the video and expressed that they hoped we would make it. That was probably a common sentiment of many, although others did not convey it quite so bluntly.

We went to Evanston for our honeymoon, nothing too fancy or expensive, after all he had spent all of his money on the ring. On our wedding night, November 1, 1997, I took one last shot with my husband. While we were dating, I started drinking again. To mask the guilt, to try to fit in with his crowd, to do what he liked to do. I never liked it, and it definitely never liked me. I ugly cried worse than usual, and man, did it make me sick. I never understood how it was fun or attractive, and yes, I felt like that and I did it anyway. We were given a gift set containing a fifth of whiskey and two shot glasses. I downed my glass then promised Scott that I would never drink again. He was good with it as he would not need to share his alcohol and could have a permanent designated driver.

Scott and I purchased an old single wide. We gutted it and remodeled with new sheetrock, cupboards, bathroom fixtures, and carpet. We put it on a rental lot that was only a block down the road from my mom. She had broken her neck at work, was on workers' comp, was fighting for disability, and recovering from neck surgery. It was handy that she was just up the road from us. Especially when we learned that we would be needing even more help with the kids. I started on the pill even though my chances of getting pregnant were cut in half. Not only did I get pregnant on the honeymoon anyway, but with twins.

I knew a girl from high school that was having twins also. She shared her doctor's information with me, so I decided to go to Kemmerer, Wyoming, the same place she was going. Because Scott was working in construction, he ended up getting laid off for the winter. I had been on WIC and Medicaid before as a single mom and knew it could help carry us through. We did qualify for the assistance, and what a blessing that turned out to be. After a few months, Scott ended up getting a job as an ironworker. However, at the time, if you qualified for services, you were eligible for a full year even if your financial situation improved.

The twins were due in August, and even with the ultrasound, we never could get a good look at both of them. We knew baby A was a girl, but baby B was more modest and never let us identify their gender. It looked as if there were two sacks, so we were thinking and Scott was hoping for a boy and a girl. If I had learned one thing, it was that life doesn't always turn out how you hope. At the end of the first week in June, I started going into labor. We rounded up a sitter for the kids, then Scott and my mom rushed me to Kemmerer.

After assessing the situation, they injected me with medication that was supposed to suppress labor. It did not work as intended; I felt like I had been doused with lighter fluid and set on fire. I started simultaneously throwing up and wetting my pants. Scott may have been panicking on the inside. The hospital was not equipped to handle premature infants. Mom, Scott, and I were transported to Evanston, Wyoming, via ambulance. There we were transferred to a jet and life flighted to the Denver, Colorado airport where I was then taken to the hospital in Denver on a helicopter, and Scott and my mom arrived in a taxi. Scott has always joked that my mom hosed him out of a helicopter ride. I was heavily sedated and vaguely remember any of it.

The hospital in Denver specialized in preemies and multiples. They just so happened to be contracted with Wyoming Medicaid at the time. Scott had to get back to work, and we needed my mom more at home watching three-and-a-half-year-old Saxen and one-and-a-half year-old Skyler. I was in good hands at the hospital; not much they could have done for me there except watch and wait. The plan was for me to receive medication in order to keep the babies inside as long as possible and to give me injections that would aid in the twins' lung development. I could have potentially been there for up to two months getting them to term. After a week, one of the longest weeks of my life up till that point, my water broke. The doctors agreed not to induce labor, but they would not prolong it either. Scott and Mom had to make the seven-hour drive and pray they would make it in time.

We had learned that we were having two girls. It was not until my water broke that we discovered that the embryonic sack was connected, and our girls were identical. Baby A was going to be named JoDee. I had always liked that name and wished it for myself. If baby B was a boy, he would have been named John Wayne; Scott's middle name is Wayne, and he always wanted to be named John. We had to come up with another girl's name, fast. Scott was passionate about hunting and guns. We started listing gun names, and I wanted Pistol Page, but we figured they would call her PP, and we couldn't have that. We started listing gun parts and landed on Trigger. My grandma Walker pleaded with us to name her Jane and not put Trigger on the birth certificate, but we didn't listen. Others thought she was named after Roy Rogers horse, but she was not.

Scott and Mom made it in time to be gowned up and escorted to the delivery room. They had to prep me as if I was going to have a c-section in case the delivery went sideways as with twins there is a greater probability of that happening. Thankfully, I did not require one. JoDee Lynne was born four pounds, thirteen ounces and placed in my arms; a minute and a half later, Trigger Jane was born at four pounds, five ounces and handed right to her dad. He was emotional and immediately bonded. While transporting the babies to the NIC unit, Scott's parents arrived and ran into us in the hall. They were amazed that I was up and walking around so soon.

Susan, my same friend that was at my other two births, was now living in Laramie and made the trip to Denver to visit us.

I thought the long week in the hospital was bad. It was nothing compared to the next four weeks. I had to leave my babies in Denver, seven hours away. JoDee for two weeks before we got to take her home, and Trigger had to stay an additional two weeks. It was torture abandoning her. When they were both there, at least they had each other. Leaving her alone felt unnatural for me. I hated every minute of it but rationalized that she was in good care and staying there was her best chance at survival. We did go back and forth a few times to check in and see the girls. Once we got both of them home, it felt much better. Saxen and Skyler each had a sister to take care of, and they were both so much help; I needed their help.

Scott was working long hours, and I had four kids, the oldest being three. My mom and Grandma Walker came and lent a hand with the children. Saxen and Skyler pitched in with feeding, changing, and fetching items for me. I had to pump, measure, feed, and document everything to make sure the twins were eating and thriving. Since they were premature, we had to limit their contact with people and germs, but we were cautious and still had visitors. The kids were so much fun, and I enjoyed getting them all dressed up for an unreasonable number of pictures. The twins were about four months old when they started sleeping through the night—a much-needed tender mercy for me.

Time flew by, and before we knew it, it was our anniversary.

CHAPTER TEN

Another Birth

WE SURVIVED OUR FIRST YEAR of marriage, although it was not without difficulties. We sold our first trailer and purchased two acres out of town with a single-wide on it that we also remodeled and updated. The property had a beautiful view of the Uinta mountains and a river below the hill. We had hoped to build a home there one day. This piece of land was located in The Church of Jesus Christ of Latter-day Saints, Lyman 4th ward, the same one I lived in when my sister died. My father-in-law happened to be the bishop of that ward at the time and was now my bishop.

I started feeling the nudge to get active in church again. Scott was also making comments about getting the kids to church, even though he had no intentions of attending himself. I delayed having the twins blessed at church for lots of reasons; they were premature, we were staying away from crowds, and I was torn over my sinful situation. I had delayed Skyler's blessing as well, and we finally had the three of them blessed together in Grandpa Allen's home where he gave all three of them a name and a blessing in conjunction with the girls' first birthday celebration.

I knew that I had sinned and needed to take care of it through the process of repentance. Given the severity of my actions, one of the steps included confessing to *my* bishop— my father-in-law.

It seemed to me that Allen had changed for the better over the years. He was one of my high school teachers, and I did not care for him or my husband then. They both liked to joke and tease, and I was raised in a very tense household; I did not find them funny. I thought they were rude.

Luckily, I had changed a lot since high school as well. I finally mustered up enough courage to confess and start the repentance process. The second time was different as I had made temple covenants, and therefore, the process required extra steps. One of those steps included being disfellowshipped. That meant that I could not take the sacrament, pray, or hold a calling. I was asked to read several recommended books, including the Book of Mormon, and encouraged to attend church and all of my other meetings. I looked forward to Gospel Doctrine class and studying all of the principals that I had missed learning previously.

As time passed, I started getting more eager to return to the temple. The one place where I could feel peace and quiet. With four children and a husband that was sometimes more of a child than a partner, I was struggling. He was drinking and "playing" with his friends. He had continued ironworking, and that was taking him out of town a lot. I was reluctant to lean on my husband fully as I was still not sure if we were going to make it.

I was praying and asking God, "Why?" Why did He want me with this man, if he was not going to live the gospel with me. I fasted and prayed monthly, to see if I should leave him.

My prayers were answered at church through a member of the Relief Society presidency. She taught and bore her testimony about how she waited on her husband for twenty plus years; he finally came around, and they were now married in the temple. I was inspired to keep pressing forward with very little faith. I did not see how my husband was going to get from where he was, to where I wanted him to be.

In the meantime, I got pregnant again, with twins, again. We were already bursting at the seams in our three bed, one bath trailer. I started going back to Kemmerer, and my doctor wanted to get ahead of any possible difficulties. Three months in, I started to cramp and spot. Which resulted in a doctor visit, where an ultrasound revealed only one heartbeat. I lost one baby, and the other survived. I received a priesthood blessing and was comforted when told that ALL was happening in accordance with God's will. I should have guessed how stubborn the remaining child would be. Not only did she hang on, but she did not want to come out. I went two weeks over my due date before they decided to induce me. Once everything got started, labor went fast. So fast in fact, that I did not have time to receive the requested epidural. It freaking hurt, but once they placed Spring, at six pounds, seven ounces in my arms, the pain faded away.

Scott picked out Spring Ann's name. He said, "We should have had her in the Spring, what kind of idiot has a kid during hunting season?" She finally arrived in mid-October 2000. Scott asked my permission to go hunting instead of being at the delivery. Not only did I not give my permission, but threatened him if he missed it, and reminded him that he was "the idiot." My mom, Jane, and Scott were there. This was the first time Susan was not in the room or at the hospital. Later, Allen brought the other four kids over to see and hold their new baby sister. They were so excited and attentive to her.

I always wanted a lot of children, but throughout and after that pregnancy, I knew I could not do it anymore. Plus, I already had my hands full, five kids under the age of six, it was very hectic. Scott and I both decided to be done. To ensure that we would be, Scott went and had a vasectomy. Within six months, it became necessary that I have a hysterectomy as well. Scott realized he shouldn't have rushed his procedure and stated that it was like getting kicked in the genitalia, *twice*.

I was having health issues and trying to navigate a less-than-ideal marriage and maintain mine and the kids' activity in the church. Scott was a good dad and friend and I loved him. I was envious that I did not receive the same time and attention as the more important people and things on his priority list. I was used to him being gone a lot with his several hobbies and shift work; he had secured employment out at the mines. It was a blessing for our family financially, and he was not required to go out of town like with his last job. We all missed him when he was gone. His rotating schedule was an adjustment for us all. Most of the time, I felt like a single parent. I was hard on him. I frequently complained about him not being more available. I needed more help. When he wasn't working, he made sure that he got to hunt, drink, play, golf, ride horses, go snow machining, camping, and hang out with his friends. He had made a comment that he was "training me." I thought, *two can play that game.*

I had my temple recommend back for a while and tried to go here and there. Although, it was hard to fit it into my life with everything that was going on. When I renewed my recommend on Sunday, February 11, 2001, I decided that I would go to the temple every month. I had a discussion with Scott about my desire, and that I would need his cooperation to achieve it. I reminded him that he was able to do all of the things that were important to him and that this was important to me, so he agreed to help.

My journal entry from that time reads,

"My greatest, most righteous desire is to be sealed for time and eternity to Scott and the kids. I don't want to be without them. If I even make it (I hope so). I have made a lot of bad choices in my life and have a lot of regrets, but I feel I have taken care of these things with the Lord. I hoped and felt that He had forgiven me. I hope that He will continue to forgive me, as I know I will make a lot more mistakes in my life before it's over."

I purposely omitted the struggles from my journals. I did not know about manifesting things in writing at the time. I just didn't want my kids to read all the bad stuff after I died. I wanted them to know that I loved them and their dad. I wanted to overlook the bad and focus on the love.

It took me years to bring myself to read my sister's diary. I felt like I was invading her privacy. Once I did read it, it was less than satisfying. It contained normal teenage girl thoughts. "I love so-and-so. Me and so-and-so forever." Several of that same entry with rotating boy names. However, it also contained real feelings such as, "I hate my annoying little sister." I knew I was irritating at times like all siblings are. It was heartbreaking to me that all of those blank pages would never be filled with how I outgrew it, that she forgave me, and later we became best friends... they would remain blank, empty, unresolved, final.

My husband knew and hung out with my sister. He spent time with her at church, outdoor activities, and at the motorcycle track. Actually, my husband and my father-in-law were identified as being out by the Gas-N-Go the day my sister's body was found. I did not know that until after we were married. They had been sighting in their guns and later questioned by law enforcement. They had no information to add to the investigation. Over the years, random people would try to encourage reopening the case after they had been to a physic or read books about other crimes that had been going on in our area in the early eighties. I knew from my patriarchal blessing that I would not know the truth until after the resurrection, when all truth will be revealed. I had a family and did not want to spend my time and energy stirring up the past; it was not going to bring her back.

After Saxen inconceivably fell out of her crib at three months old, I transitioned the rest of my children from a bassinet straight to a toddler bed. I figured if they were going to fall, it was better to fall twelve inches, not thirty-six. On May 18, 2001, when Spring was seven months old, my theory was overturned. That particular evening Scott was at a golf tournament. My mom was visiting from Vernal, where she had been living and helping her parents. We had not seen her in a while, so the kids wanted her to stay the night. We put Spring to bed at 8:45 p.m., then watched a movie. I was in the bathroom brushing my teeth about 11:30 p.m. JoDee was the last child awake and was going to sleep in my bed.

She went to get in but immediately returned and asked, "Where is Spring?"

"She is in bed," I replied.

She informed me that Spring was not there. I rushed into the room to find an empty toddler bed. I went out to the couch and asked my mom if she moved Spring, she said she did not.

We both sprinted back down the hall and flipped on the light to find her. I saw her little feet sticking up from a small hole by the headboard. I lifted her out by her foot. She was grey, blue, and purple, her face was swollen, and she was not breathing. Mom immediately grabbed her away from me and told me to call 911. I called while she started CPR. The cops and ambulance arrived, and I rode with Spring to the emergency room. My brother and his second wife came and stayed with the kids.

Mom had her breathing before the EMTs arrived, but they took her to be evaluated anyway. After my brother arrived, Mom drove over to the hospital. They did X-rays to look for neck and lung damage. Spring was in good health, and everything checked out fine. I requested a blessing at the hospital, and the missionaries came and blessed her.

They said, "Her loved ones here on earth and her loved ones that have passed on were all watching over her and that she had a special mission here on earth and that her Father in Heaven would make sure that she could complete that mission."

I recorded it in my journal verbatim. I believed that one of those loved ones on the other side was my sister. I was thankful for her, JoDee, and for my mom, and that she just so happened to be there. I was grateful and relieved that it was not God's will for Spring to leave at that time.

I was called to be an advisor over the Mia-Maid's, a young women's group in The Church of Jesus Christ of Latter-day Saints, for ages fourteen to sixteen. I taught a lesson for the second time ever. The first time I taught was before I joined the military. I did it as a favor for a close family friend. I was not even active at the time. For my new calling, I planned, studied, and prepared, but it all just came out wrong. Even with that said, I guess it was okay, and I survived it. I hoped to keep improving and one day be good at it. I was excited to work with the girls and have a chance as a leader to complete the Young Women's Program. It was something I did not participate in as a youth. Satan was working hard on me to give up. I lacked confidence in myself but trusted that Heavenly Father would continue to help me as long as I kept trying.

At the end of January 2001, the kids and I made a trip to Vernal to see my mom and my grandparents, who were not doing well, and I didn't know how much longer they were going to have. I hated to watch them suffer from emphysema and struggle for every breath they took. I wondered what Heavenly Father's purpose was for prolonging their life. I had come to believe that God was in control of life and death. That when it is your time to go, you will. I know God knows all the answers, even if we don't. Both my grandparents spent a lot of time at the bar when they were younger. My grandpa started smoking at eight years old. I am not sure when my grandma started, but I have a picture of her smoking when she was fifteen. Even if she started then, that is still young. My mom had different parents than I ever knew. They came to our house and saw Spring after she was born. That was the last trip they made over the mountain together.

The evening we came home from that trip to Vernal we were greeted at the door by Scott. He was eager to see us and surprised us with a candlelight dinner. The table was already set and the meal dished up. He had baked cheesy bread and homemade chili, using one can of every kind of bean in the house. It was actually good. That was the first time he had displayed such thoughtfulness. I was surprised and touched by it; his act of kindness definitely went in the journal.

I ended my entry with, "Scott doing something that sweet had never entered my mind. It will leave a lasting impression in my heart of how sweet and wonderful of a man the Lord has blessed me with. Thank you, Scott, I think you are wonderful."

CHAPTER ELEVEN

The Grandparents I Knew

I LOVED GRANDMA AND GRANDPA MCMICKELL, we were close. Grandma crocheted while having conversations and creating beautiful handmade artwork. Grandpa was an all-around handyman and skilled mechanic. He could tell you what was wrong with your car based on your description of the noise it was making. Most people change as they get older, I think. They figure some things out in life and soften or settle down. Sometimes people decide to shake things up and become wild and experimental. My grandparents were the former. I was told stories about their partying days and how much time they spent at the bar, but I never knew them like that. I didn't deal with the drinking, the yelling, and my grandma's need for perfection. She was patient with me as I spent hours painting her nails, brushing, fixing, and playing with her hair. I was told my grandpa stood six foot three inches tall, but I didn't know him until after he was injured when a semi drove through their camper. He required back surgery that left him slightly hunched and shorter.

Their fifth wheel was restored, and Grandpa pulled it everywhere with his old orange pickup. We used to lay on the bed and look out the window above the truck cab and watch the scenery go by as he drove us over the mountain from Vernal, Utah, to Bridger Valley, Wyoming, and back again. He hauled it on camping trips, fishing trips, and extended visits; it was their second home. Grandpa loved to take everyone fishing. We would go stay on the Green River and spend days on the bank. He kept all the poles in the water for the grandkids, baiting our hooks, untangling our line, teaching us how to cast and reel. One year my uncle left his pole unattended. It was cast in the water next to mine. He got a bite, and it pulled the rod off the forked stick holder, so I ran and grabbed it and reeled it in. It was the biggest catfish I'd ever seen. I was proud and took ownership for the catch. We ate fried catfish and rainbow trout; Grandpa would eat their cooked eyeballs and suck out their brains, *gross*. It didn't stop me from playing with his false teeth and putting his set of teeth in my mouth. My mom has a picture somewhere.

The hardest I have laughed was when we were playing dice at their kitchen table. It was either Yahtzee, or bloop; we played them both regularly. Grandma Sue opened her mouth to speak, and her top denture fell down. It was the funniest thing, and we couldn't stop laughing. It seemed like most of the family had lost their natural teeth or were on their way to doing so. I was afraid of losing my teeth, so I put extra effort into caring for them. I didn't realize that there are multiple factors that go into determining dental health, and oral hygiene is just one of them.

I can still see their house after they converted the garage into the kitchen and dining area and turned the old kitchen into the new master bedroom. The front door opened into the living room. On the immediate right was the doorway to enter into the dining room, with the kitchen to the south toward the laundry room. It had a door leading to the large back yard and garden. There were tall apartment buildings behind their house, and a man used to stand naked in his window and expose himself while us kids were outside playing.

We spent many nights out on the lawn with flashlights collecting earthworms to keep the bait stocked. Grandma would let me take the salt and pepper shaker out to the garden, and I would sit and eat fresh tomatoes like you would an apple. Next to the garden was a big, broken-down yellow bus used as a shed. It was stacked with boxes of prized possessions.

Grandma Sue and Grandpa would accompany us on our family treasure hunting adventures. Grandma always looked for arrowheads and had quite the collection. She contributed to my love of gathering pretty rocks. One time while out adventuring, we were driving on a dirt road with deep ruts. Our family was split between two vehicles, and my sister and I were riding with Grandma and Grandpa. Mom, Dad, and the others were in the car ahead of us.

Terri was eating licorice; she put one red Twizzlers in each nostril and verbally got everyone's attention. Grandpa shifted his eyes off the road and turned to look. He didn't see that my dad had stopped just in front of him, and we ran into the back of his vehicle. It gave us all a good jolt.

On the left side of their living room was an opening to a small hall that gave access to two bedrooms, the bathroom, and the converted master bedroom. Their tub, sink, and toilet were aqua in color. I enjoyed taking baths in the deep tub to get rid of the fish, dirt, and worm smells and play in the bubbles. I would dress up in a Treecko fabric nightgown and matching sheer robe, holding my serving tray full of goodies, playing princess waitress, and serving everyone treats.

We crafted, sewed, and colored with the Artex paints. My grandpa didn't participate all of the time, but he would craft, paint, and quilt with us on occasion. Grandma taught me how to crochet, but most of the time, I just enjoyed her work because crocheting made me tense. She made me earmuffs that looked like roses, dolls, pillow dolls, a doll with the blanket attached, miniature dolls with a convertible house bag, and knockoff Strawberry Shortcake dolls. I still have Cookie and Sherbet; and I still cuddle under my reversible pastel and white striped afghan she made for me when I was fourteen.

Grandpa liked to be outside tinkering, doing mechanics, or anything with his hands. He could fix anything, and everyone would send their stuff to him to get it repaired. He loved to serve others in that way. My grandma joked that when she needed him to do something of hers, she would give it to her sister-in-law to give to him; it was the quickest way to get it back. Long before it became popular on social media, my grandpa would let me pick his pimples for hours at a time. I think I already mentioned how tolerant and patient he was. Grandpa would eat anything but corned beef. He said he ate enough of that in the service. He always had to have clean socks and would go through a couple pairs a day; later I learned it was for his jungle rot. When I was in the service, I asked him if he had to kill anyone in the war. Heavy-hearted, he said yes. He conveyed his traumatic experiences which I will not repeat here, but after watching the movie, *Saving Private Ryan*, he said the only thing missing was the stench.

He did not miss that smell, but the scents I miss are his Old Spice products and aftershave. He always had Carmex in his pocket and on his lips. I miss the familiar whiff of grease or fish on his hands. I will never forget the aroma of coffee that always filled their home. I do not miss the cigarette smoke. When you are around it all of the time, you're desensitized, but my grandma never got used to it. Even though she smoked, she always hated the smell. She was embarrassed by it until receiving counsel from a bishop that helped her feel less self-conscious. He had been inviting her to come to church, and she expressed her concern for her smoky fragrance.

He told her, "Kenna Sue, if every sin had an odor, we would not be able to meet as a congregation." It is true, everyone struggles with something, some are just more noticeable than others.

I detected that Grandma and Grandpa had their share of troubles in life. They were more open about their family stories than my dad's parents were, and both of their upbringings were difficult. I suppose only God fully understood their difficulties. They shared interesting, sad, tragic stories. Grandpa dropped out of school when he was eight or nine to care for his siblings, but inevitably the state came and split them up and took them away. He got his high school equivalency and was sent to the Korean war. My grandma's dad passed away when she was an infant, and her stepdad was abusive. One of her three brothers was killed in Korea. Her widowed mother lived just up the road from her, and they did not always get along.

After my mom's brother, Michael Dee, passed away from injuries sustained from a car accident, the hospital staff asked if he would be an organ donor. My grandparents declined. Later a nurse told Grandma, "It was so nice of you to donate your son's eyes."

My grandma spent the rest of her life looking into people's eyes to see if they were her son's distinct crystal blue ones. I found it a bit strange until I became a mother, then I got it. What people say can have a big impact on us. A seemingly simple comment, probably well intended, can stick with us and alter how we think, feel, or behave. I was little when Uncle Michael Dee passed away and barely remember it, but Mom always said that Terri would talk about him and tell the family that she needed to die when she was young so he would remember her.

My grandparents made me feel special; they spent time with me, engaged with me, and loved me. I remember them parking the fifth wheel at our house and staying for extended periods of time. My grandparents used to own the single-wide we lived in, the one that was relocated so many times I lost count. They ended up selling it to my parents and moving back to Vernal. Some of my favorite memories were in that trailer. When they came for Christmas, our family spent hours playing with our new toys and electronics. Atari was the all-time favorite, Pac Man and Space Invaders were the best. Most of the time the kids would have to beg the adults to share and let us have a turn. I hoped when I grew up that I would have that much fun with my own family.

After I was honorably discharged from the Navy, I would spend my Fourth of July's in Vernal with my grandparents. Grandpa was proud of me and signed me up as the youngest female in the VFW at the time. I rode on a float with him on several occasions. A few of those times, the years they honored Gold Star Families, my great-grandma Marell rode as well. One of my favorite parts was feeling the vibrations from the Hill Air Force Base jets as they flew over to kick off the parade. They had stopped throwing candy there, so the crowd just cheered and waved small flags. It was very patriotic and humbling. I appreciate all who have served, especially my grandpa, knowing his backstory.

The first trailer Scott and I remodeled we purchased from Grandma and Grandpa. I'm not sure why they bought it in the first place, but those plans fell through, so it worked out for Scott and me. My grandma worried about me and my happiness; given my history I didn't blame her. She told me about a dream that she had and shared that she knew I was going to be all right, and that I would be very "content" with Scott. Her dream put her worries to ease but caused me to reconsider. I didn't understand the true meaning until much later, so I interpreted it to mean that I had settled. Sometimes it felt like that, like I was forgoing my dreams, as our lives did not look like I had envisioned; although, we did have lots of fun like I had always hoped my family would.

After my grandparents passed away, I was allowed to go into the yellow bus storage unit and go through all the boxes. It was not filled with valuable treasures—just so much junk, paperwork, and things. It made me sad to think that they had held onto that stuff for years and for what? So, I would have to go through it and throw it away. There were a few things that I did keep, including a green Tiara glass luncheon set. I took it home, washed them, and started using them for tea parties with my kids, which was their intended purpose. I remember thinking what good are our "things" if we don't use or enjoy them. Little did I know that dejunking the bus was just the beginning.

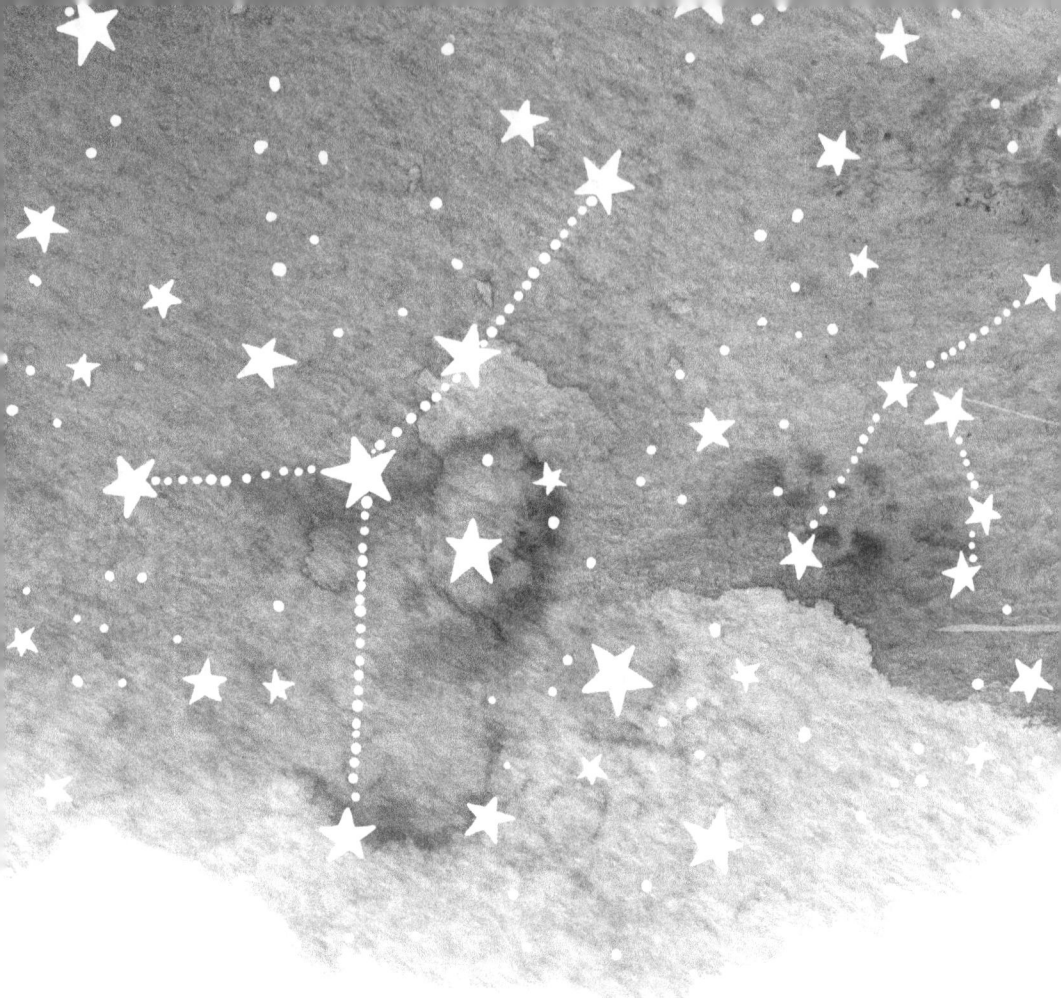

Re·con·cep·tion

A new or different idea of what something or someone is like, or a new or different basic understanding of a situation or a principle.

CHAPTER TWELVE

New Beginnings

WE HAD MORE THAN OUTGROWN our second trailer and were not in a position to start building. We found a four bedroom, two bath house for sale that was in our budget. As a bonus, it was in our same ward boundaries. The sellers wanted one last Christmas in the house with their newly returned missionary before turning it over to us. Everything was in order at the bank, and we agreed on a timeline. We were so eager to get into our new house and leave the single-wide and septic issues behind. Unfortunately, the marital problems were still packed up and hauled with us.

The house was built in 1978. It retained some original brown paneling, olive-green appliances, and discolored shag carpet. Most of the walls were covered in wallpaper of varying colors and designs. My least favorite was the northwest downstairs bedroom. It had bright blue carpet and matching trim with cream wallpaper covered in geese with the same blue colored spots and bows around their necks. The only thing that would have made them worse would have been if they were wearing bonnets. With time and consistent effort, I worked on redecorating our home. I was still trying to work on myself, my husband, and our marriage. More incidents were omitted from the pages of my journal. I did not want proof that they took place. I did not realize until years later that they were still documented. Not on paper but written in my subconscious.

I was very stressed and anxious all of the time. Scott would stumble in at two or three in the morning, and after worrying about him for hours, I was relieved that he was alive. However, immediately after relief came anger and frustration. I was unaware in the first several years of marriage that it was a waste of time to try and have a conversation or reason with a drunk person. Our worst fights were when he was drinking, and I hated it. The following mornings, I would still be mad, but he never remembered why. He was not the same person when he was drunk. He was not wonderful. He always liked to joke and tease, but alcohol took it to an unacceptable level. Oftentimes, he was passed out by seven o'clock at night, in the middle of the floor. The kids would play on him like a jungle gym; they were oblivious to his patient condition.

On a handful of occasions, I considered getting wasted just to show Scott what I was dealing with, for him to see things from my perspective. I rationalized a perfect outcome resulting in him realizing that he needed to quit drinking. The more I pondered on it, I always concluded that the lesson would be lost on him and backfire on me; the only thing he would get out of it was that I broke my promise to never drink again. I could see the fault in my plan and how it would be unsuccessful. Eventually, I completely abandoned that idea.

I had a bad habit of ruining my life; it only took about fifteen minutes in my head. I would imagine us getting a divorce, splitting up our property. I had even figured out how we would handle shared custody of the kids. I wrote it all out once on a lined piece of paper divided right down the middle like we would be.

I wrote, "I would rather be alone than always come last. The kids and I deserve more. You obviously don't want the same things I want for us. Let me find someone who does, and you can live as you please without hurting me and the children." I threatened divorce frequently. He would tell me, "I am not going to let you get rid of me."

I'm sure he could have lived without me. He would not have been able to live without the kids. My hopes, dreams, and disappointments were like a yo-yo he was controlling. He showed glimpses of improvement and often said he would do better. When he wasn't working, he would get my expectations up to go with me to family or church activities, but by time they arrived, he backed out or was too inebriated to attend. So many plans were canceled and events attended solo or just me and the kids.

Once, when just the kids and I returned home from an event, one of them was having an absolute meltdown. I was frazzled when I pulled our white suburban into the garage, slammed it into park, closed the garage door, and told the rest of the children to go into the house and get ready for bed. I picked up the one child and carried them kicking and screaming to their room. The next morning when Scott got home from graveyards, he woke me up and inquired as to why I had left the vehicle running all night. I had no idea that I had even left the SUV on. We could smell the carbon monoxide in the house; we had to open all of the windows and doors to air it out. I could have accidentally killed my family while in my worn-out state.

I beat myself up for the incident for quite some time. However, I had other ideas and feelings as a result that lasted much longer. I started having intrusive thoughts when I would pull into the garage. Thoughts that would encourage me to sit in there with my children, with the car running. I could end all of the pain and suffering. I could save them from a hard life. We would all be together; it would solve all of our issues and such. I fought those feelings alone for almost three years. I could not tell anyone. They would put me in the nuthouse and take away my children, and Scott would leave me for sure. I put a strategy in place to always prepare all occupants for a quick exit out of the car and into the house. I would make sure the vehicle was shut off, and I never lingered.

I also did not disclose that I lived in fear of everyone dying on me. I would send my husband to work and envision that being the last time I would get to hug him goodbye, the last time I would see him alive. When he was out late or didn't come home on time, I just knew he was in a wreck and dead in a ditch somewhere. Getting each of my children past the age of fifteen was mentally strenuous for me.

I would tell God, "If You are going to take them from me, just do it already." The anticipation was torture. I had every detail of their funerals planned. None of my conceived scenarios ever involved me dying, just everyone around me. I was always the one left behind to pick up and manage the shattered pieces.

Some broken pieces are easier to handle than others. By April 2002, my grandma Sue was mostly bed ridden. However, she was partaking of the sacrament and did all of the work necessary to secure a recommend for herself. She was concerned how she was going to move around the temple to perform the initiatory and endowment. God answered her prayers through others, a friend from her ward, my mom, and me. In between obtaining her recommend and attending the temple, she passed away. Because she had received her own recommendation prior to her passing, we were able to go and do her work before the funeral. The spiritual experience continued as we prepared her physical body for burial. My mother and I dressed her in all white clothing. I did her hair, makeup, and painted her nails as I often did when she was alive; it was a very sacred experience.

My grandpa was heartbroken. They had been together just over fifty years. He spent the next several months working toward and obtaining his own temple recommend. I was able to participate with him being sealed to Grandma and some of their children for time and all eternity. Families are like links in a chain, and Heavenly Father wants us all welded together and linked to Him. It bonds us on both sides of the veil and breaks the bands of death. I did not understand that when my sister died. When she passed, I learned the brutal reality of death, and the gaping hole it leaves in your existence. Having a testimony of God's plan of happiness helps fill that void with love and hope. That was what I was able to feel when my grandpa crossed over just seven short months after his wife. Although knowing and believing makes it bearable, it does not make it pain free.

Along with the grief and mental health issues I was experiencing, I was simultaneously having several physical difficulties as well. I had chronic fatigue, constant abdominal pain, stomach problems, frequent sinus infections, and headaches. I finally received a diagnosis of IBS after several years of suffering. With my new verdict, I went through the long process and met the qualifications to receive an increase to my VA disability. I had a lot of anxiety living with and managing my health. My situation increased my stress and added extra steps to everything I was already doing. Poor health affected my quality of life and hindered my desire to participate in or even enjoy a variety of activities.

I continued to pray and counsel Heavenly Father. I murmured and complained about my hard situation to God, my husband, and my new bishop. With Scott and my bishop, I left out the crazy thoughts I was having, but God knew. Scott never took anything seriously. He did not like to discuss feelings and thought that everything was always wonderful. He would mock my concerns desiring improvement or change.

After a few times of intermittently talking to my bishop, he told me, "Heavenly Father could take all of this away, but He is not going to." I left his office disappointed that all of my problems were not going to be solved in one fail swoop. At first, I thought it was rude of him, but after time and much consideration, I eventually found his advice helpful.

I read self-help books and would implement suggested tips and tricks. I received lots of priesthood blessings. I continued attending the temple and taking the kids to church. Allen and Jane assisted me along with another special family in our ward. The mom and her girls helped me tremendously. They consistently came to my aid making it so much easier on me. Another woman in our ward would always share the advice she gave to her own daughter, not knowing that it was helping me as well.

At that time, I was encouraged by a sister to sing in relief society. I was in the mode of saying yes to all opportunities, as if it were from God. I do not have a great voice, and I cannot read music, but I love to sing and I agreed to do it anyway; turns out it was a cruel joke. At that same time, I was assigned to speak in sacrament the week after my vocal performance.

One blessing that came from the whole experience was that I was so worried about the singing that preparing and giving the talk seemed like the easier task.

I spent a great deal of time practicing the Christmas song I selected. My kids and I could all recite it word for word. We would sing and dance around the kitchen, like I used to do with my mom growing up. We laughed and enjoyed it as I had always hoped we would. I exposed my kids to lots of types of music as well. Music and dancing were fun activities in our home. A sign hangs on my wall, it reads, "This kitchen is for dancing." I would often sing to my kids at bedtime with my "mother voice," you know the one your kids love because they don't know any better. One of my kids favorites I would sing was Cindy Lauper's, "Time After Time," I know it by heart. That song, along with "You are my Sunshine" and "I Am a Child of God" were my go-to songs. I intended for my kids to know how much they were loved, although I was not always kind and dear.

I yelled frequently as I had learned. It was one weakness that I was actively working on. I didn't want to; I did not admire that attribute about myself. I used to explain to my children that we can love someone and not like what they do. On occasion I would say, through gritted teeth, I love you, but I do not like how you are behaving right now. Once while using my loud, frustrated, mom voice, my youngest said, "Mom, I love you, but I do not like you screaming at us right now."

I immediately shrank. I apologized as I did often, and with lots of prayers and forgiveness, over time, I continued to improve. As my kids have grown, they retell stories and we laugh, but I wish I could have become better sooner. Sometimes the little things take longer to overcome than the big ones do. I learned that the atonement of Jesus Christ is not a one-time gig. You can use it again and again, as many times as it takes, for as long as it takes, in order to overcome our weaknesses.

After about six years of functioning in this stressful manner, Scott and I decided that neither of us wanted to continue that way. I eventually convinced him to sit down and have a hard conversation. I needed to decide that if he never stopped drinking and never went to church, if I could live with that. He needed to decide if I was not going to get taller, thinner, blonder, or grow bigger boobs, and stop yelling, all of the things he would fix about me, did he want to stick it out. We asked ourselves and one another, did we love each other enough, exactly how we were, to keep trying and stay married. What we were doing was not working, and something needed to change.

After that discussion, we decided that we did love each other enough, and that we would both do and be better. A shift happened for me. I stopped focusing on all the things that he was not doing and acknowledged all of the good things he was doing. I let go of my flawed personal agenda, changed my expectations, and started to concentrate on what I could do and what was in my control—me. I wanted to enjoy the life that I actually had, not live in disappointment because life was not what I thought it should look like.

CHAPTER THIRTEEN

The Shift

I HAD FOUND A QUOTE that encouraged me to alter my
thoughts and actions. It reads,

If I really want to improve my situation
I can work on the one thing over
which I have control—myself.
I can stop trying to shape up my husband,
or my friends, and work on my own weakness.
I can focus on being a great marriage partner or a
great co-worker or a good neighbor,
a source of unconditional love and support.
Hopefully, those around me will feel the power of
proactive example and respond
in kind. But whether anyone does
or doesn't, the most positive way I can
influence my own situation
is to work on myself, on my being.

– UNKNOWN

This quote unknowingly became my new motto. It wasn't easy, but I tried to make a continuous effort to work on myself. I remember watching a commercial one day as I was lying on the couch. It stated that not exercising was the equivalent of smoking two packs of cigarettes a day. My husband was chewing and I did not care for it. I would make smart remarks such as, "Hurry and kiss me while you still have a lip."

However, Scott was physically fit and could run circles around me. I was impressed with the thought that drinking and chewing were "Word of Wisdom" issues. If you are not familiar with that principle, it is found in the 89th section of the Doctrine and Covenants of The Church of Jesus Christ of Latter-day Saints. It outlines the do's and don'ts for our physical bodies, and if we heed this counsel, we are promised both temporal and spiritual blessings.

Although I was abstaining from the recommended substances to avoid, such as coffee, strong drink, and tobacco, I realized I, too, had Word of Wisdom issues. Many church talks included ideas and recommendations that can fall under the Word of Wisdom umbrella. Such as moderation in all things. Don't sleep too much or overeat, and we should exercise and take care of our bodies. I overslept, over ate, and did not exercise. I knew that I was not where I wanted or needed to be.

I continued serving in callings, attending the temple, reading the scriptures, praying, and having family home evenings. I spoke in sacrament and the adult session of Stake Conference. Every time I did, I felt the Spirit throughout the process of preparing and delivering what God wanted me to say. My confidence grew in my ability and in trusting that Heavenly Father was aiding me along the way. I knew that I was nothing without Him and acknowledged His hand in strengthening me. I gave Him the credit for all things. I could tell the difference throughout the week when I attended church, and I could tell the difference throughout the month because of my time in the temple.

One Sunday morning, I was struggling to get out of bed and said, "Maybe I won't go to church today."

Scott inquired, "Didn't you say that your whole week goes better when you go to church?"

"Yes, yes it does." I drug myself out of bed, then to church.

I became very aware that my husband was watching and listening to me. I felt a responsibility to be a good example to him and the kids. I could also feel Satan doubling his efforts to break me. I had to reverse my line of thinking and started asking myself, "Why would Satan not want me to do this thing, fill in the blank."

Usually because I was going to be uplifted and fortified. He did not want that for me because it was exactly what I needed. I was determined not to let him stop me in my pursuit to remain faithful. I continued to trudge forward and be strictly obedient. This resulted in our Sundays being the worst day of the week at our house. Scott and I fought more on Sundays. It seemed that he drank more on Sundays. It was definitely a day of tug-of-war between us, our misaligned behaviors and beliefs.

The kids were still young enough to go along with their mother, and it was not like they were invited to Scott's activities which usually included hunting, riding horses, motorcycles, snow machines, etc. I think he liked me and the kids going to church so he felt less guilty when he was off playing. His love for hunting did inspire testimonies in our children. We learned several Bible stories such as Daniel and the Lion's Den,

David and Goliath. But Noah's Ark was one of our favorites. We definitely loved animals, including the variety of the ones that were taxidermied in our home. The kids would include that they knew that God saved the animals from the flood while bearing their testimonies. During a sacrament meeting when my oldest daughter was young, she asked, "Mom, why do we only bear our testimonies on fast Sundays and not slow Sundays?"

That was an excellent question, and one that I could not answer in a way that would satisfy her wonderment. I had many inquiries like that myself. I asked God lots of why is this happening, what if I made different choices, what do I need to be doing?

One night, He gave me a very clear direction. In October 2004, I was asked to fill in for a Tuesday night enrichment meeting at church. They had a guest speaker from the Bridger Valley Outreach there to share the educational opportunities that they offered. It was clearly impressed upon me that I needed to further my education. On my mom's side of the family, just graduating from high school was impressive. My dad's family had a few that went to college, and they were held in higher esteem than those that did not. Scott's family were all educated, and most worked as teachers. They placed a high value on education, and out of all of us, I was the least educated.

After that night, I started looking into what it would take to transfer my military credits and get started. The only things I ever contemplated doing were being a mom, possibly a teacher, or briefly I considered a fashion designer or a model. I decided that I would take classes that would lead me to becoming a teacher.

My transfer credits came through for half of a general associate degree, and I started slow with just two classes a semester.

Scott was a trooper and supported the idea fully. He helped with the kids so I could attend classes and complete my assignments. I would accomplish my new desire not only to follow inspiration, but to obtain a college degree. I was signed up to take a Tuesday night class, but before it even started, I was called to be a leader in the Cub Scouts on Tuesday nights. I accepted and quickly rearranged my schedule.

I was insecure with my learning abilities and needed all the help I could get. I believed that in order for God to help me, I had to do everything He asked of me. So, when the Prophet asked church members in August of 2005 to read the entire Book of Mormon by the end of the year, I agreed that I would do it. I sat my kids down and invited them to read it with me, and they accepted the invitation.

"If each of you will observe this simple program [to read or reread the Book of Mormon by the end of the year], regardless of how many times you previously may have read the Book of Mormon, there will come into your lives and into your homes an added measure of the Spirit of the Lord, a strengthened resolution to walk in obedience to His commandments, and a stronger testimony of the living reality of the Son of God." ~ *Gordon B. Hinckley – Former President of The Church of Jesus Christ of Latter-day Saints.*

The kids and I started reading right away and had a nightly routine in order to meet the end of year deadline. In just a short amount of time, I was already seeing some blessings from it. September was typically a hard month for me. It was mine and Terri's birthday and the anniversary of her death. Scott always left me in September to go hunting, and it took a long time for me to realize that it triggered my abandonment issues. September of 2005 was the twentieth anniversary of my sister's passing. I often wondered how different my life would have been if she were still here, even though by this time, I had a very strong testimony of death; the timing and what happens after. I also wondered how long it would take for my husband to become active in the church. I believed that God keeps all of His promises. Scott was born under the covenant (his parents were married in the temple of The Church of Jesus Christ of Latter-day Saints) and therefore covered under that contract, but I was impatient. I loathed the disclaimer that all things happen in GOD'S timing not mine.

Scott did not accept the invitation to read with the family. He would pass through the room on occasion and linger a bit. However, at the beginning of September, he sat and listened to four chapters without leaving; I recorded it in my journal.

We got by financially, but we were broke. To be more accurate, Scott always said we were three hundred dollars negative. We were building a shop, and there was barely enough money to go around. I believed in tithing and would pay on my small disability income. I had tried to encourage him that if he would pay his tithing, he would be blessed. That month Scott decided to test the law of tithing and become a full tithe payer. The blessings rolled in. One example: we needed more gravel to finish our building project. One day I answered a knock on the door, and a man with a truckload of pea-gravel was there to deliver the load to our neighbor, but she was not home to instruct him where to dump it. He asked if we could use it, and he would bring her another load. We love tithing; it is not about money—it's about faith.

The kids and I finished reading just before Christmas. We enjoyed the holidays and the satisfaction of completion and obedience to the Prophet's challenge. Although my great grandma passed away on the 29th, we received comfort from God's plan of salvation for His children. I reminded my family that there's life after death, and that we can be with our loved ones again. On December 31 with no outside encouragement, Scott took his last dip of Copenhagen. He decided that it was time to quit, so he did. Coincidence, I think not. Our family witnessed miracles. We received promised blessings as a result of our obedience and faith. These experiences strengthened my testimony in the truthfulness of the Book of Mormon, and in the power it has in our lives as we read it. My hope in Scott and my ability to make additional changes moving forward increased.

CHAPTER FOURTEEN

Perspective

*G*ROWING UP, I was told stories about my great-grandma and how cranky she was. I learned of her odd habits and self-inflicted loneliness. We would find humor in her gift giving and retell stories of receiving cracker-jack prizes—not the box with a prize in it, just the prize after the popcorn had been eaten. We would receive cardboard cutouts of characters from cereal boxes, recycled goodie plates with the crumbs still on the empty platter. How some had to wait two years for one pair of socks as she would give them individually. She lived in Vernal, Utah, just up the road from my grandparents. After they both passed, she had no one willing to take care of her except my mom. She moved to Lyman, Wyoming, to live with my mother, and my family was able to help care for her and get to know her better. I realized that most of what I knew about my great-grandma Marell was based on the opinions of, or information from, other people.

She lived through the great depression, and as a result, acquired a frugal lifestyle. She had four children; my grandma was the youngest and the only girl. Her husband had passed away, but I never realized he was tragically killed by a boulder when my grandma Sue was only one year and ten days old. My heart broke for my great-grandma as for the first time, I started mentally putting the pieces of her life puzzle together. She was a twin, and her brother passed away when they were a few months old. She was widowed with four young children. She remarried an abusive alcoholic and chose to stay single for over twenty-four years after his passing. Her three sons were sent to war, and one never made it home from Korea. She told us that she had quietly survived breast cancer, worked as a postal clerk, and enjoyed selling Avon. She painfully expressed how she outlived and buried all of her children. I developed an appreciation and love for her. I was able to see her from a new perspective before she passed away. In The Church of Jesus Christ of Latter-day Saints, members can do temple work for our dead relatives to get their temple blessings. I was able to proxy her temple work.

One of my favorite things to do is get to know others' back stories. We usually know people where they are in life at the time and don't understand or think about how they got there. I have incorrectly made assumptions about others based on their current situation. I was later able to correct that bad habit after listening to a Stake Conference speaker. She impressed upon me that no matter how much we think we know, we never have all of the information. I was reminded of my life and how many times I had created complete puzzles about people without having all of the pieces.

Over the years, I started to gather tidbits that I did not have as a youth. I learned it was a drunk driver that caused a head on collision killing my mom's brother Michael Dee. He was the passenger, and my dad was driving and badly injured. I learned that my brother was born without a reflex valve and died three times; Grandpa Virg revived him once with CPR, the other two times were at the hospital. He had two blood transfusions, packed blood cells, and a blood exchange. He had to lay and sleep on a thirty-degree angle until he was two so he would not aspirate again. My mom lived in fear of him dying and was very protective of him. She also said she received revelation that Terri would be taken from her prior to her passing.

I was in my early twenties when I became aware that my mom had been sexually abused by her great-grandfather, locked in a dark, spider infested cellar by a mean aunt, and given alcohol from one of her uncles as an infant, to the point she could not hold up her own head. She had fears, phobias, anxiety, seasonal depression, and I am convinced that she had several other undiagnosed mental health conditions. All which contributed to her marriage, relationships, and parenting abilities. After learning these things and much more over time, I was impressed that she functioned as well as she did, considering all that she had been through.

Years into my marriage, my husband started pointing out a few abnormalities about my family dynamic that I was accustomed to. At first, I defended them. Eventually, I became more aware of inappropriate behavior and manipulation that had always been a part of my life. One day, I was watching an episode of Dr. Phil, and a mother in the middle of a divorce was telling her children that their dad did not love them. Dr. Phil reprimanded the mother, telling her that she was abusing her children. Imagine my surprise, a woman in her mid-thirties, just realizing that my mother telling me my entire life that my dad did not love me was abusive. Was there a chance it wasn't even true?

I asked my mother "Why would you tell me that my dad did not love me?"

"Because your dad asked me to tell you."

I informed her that if anything ever happened to Scott and me, and he told me to tell our children that he did not love them, they would *never* receive that message.

I did not badmouth my children's biological fathers, in their presence. It is a mother's job to protect her children, not be the person that harms them. Of course, I inquired further from my dad as well. He told me that he never said that; it was never about us kids. He loved us and tried to take us, but it was too hard to care for us while working, and we would beg and cry for our mom. That is why he stayed with her for as long as he did, *because he loved us kids*. I can only imagine his degree of difficulties. We discussed other distinct memories of mine, and he shed light and clarity on many subjects during that lengthy conversation and subsequent follow-up visits over the next several months. The information started to come together and fill in holes from my mother's stories. I was still dumb-founded as to why my own mother would hurt and confuse me with half-truths and lies. I started to question everything I thought I knew and had always been told by my mother.

After my great-grandma passed, my mother's health and well-being declined further. She barricaded herself behind mounds of boxes and junk; the hoarding started years prior, but the severity became increasingly worse after my uncle Randy, her oldest brother, passed away from cancer in October 2006. It got to where Mom could barely get off the couch. Her fentanyl patches kept her awake for days, or asleep for weeks.

I could not get a hold of her for long periods, so my biggest fear at the time was that she would pass away, and we would not immediately find her. She either could not or would not answer the door or the phone. When she finally emerged, she sometimes showed glimpses of the mother I once knew, but those occasions were few and far between.

I spoke with her doctor and expressed my concern about her overmedicated state. She was being ticketed for her yard, every other week. The extension cords she strung together almost the length of her trailer were a fire hazard as well as her broken plumbing that was draining underneath the house. Adult services, the police, and the fire marshal came to her home for an inspection and what I hoped would be an intervention. One was not provided because no children were in the home. Mom only felt more justified in her lifestyle choices, as no consequences were given. Yet, they continued to give her warnings and violations Scott and I had to fix. We were frustrated and felt alone in our fight with no assistance or backing from our government's broken system.

Scott helped me again and again as we dejunked Mom's house and yard and moved her storage piles around. He hauled items to the dump until we could no longer fit down the twelve-inch tunnel she kept recreating throughout her home. If we cleared a spot, she would fill it again. We dropped everything to go take care of her tickets she would inform us about at the last minute. Scott watched the kids when I transported her on several occasions to federal court over a two-year span. He drove us to Seattle, Washington, to drop her off at a detention center for a second mental evaluation before she could stand trial.

In Washington, after she turned herself in, Scott waited for me while I went to the temple. I recorded in my journal, "Mom is in the Lord's hands, He will watch over her. I know it will be hard, but it will be okay. I hope my mom knows how much I love her, and that I pray for her to return to her best self."

I also wrote and recorded a poem about my mother and how I felt during that time in my life.

Mother, Mother, I miss you dearly.

Mother, where have you gone?

Mother something has gone disastrously wrong, Mother...

Although you are right beside me, you are nowhere to be found.

A walking zombie using your body to get around.

Broken neck, medications, fog covering your brain.

Toxins in—reality out.

My mother, replaced with paranoia, depression, sleeping, and zoning out.

Unable to function, unable to feel, unable to reason, concentrate, or deal.

Pain and meds taken over, quality of life and teeth rotted out.

Darkness, boxes, and things piled up around you pushing everything else out.

I see what used to be my mother dragging about.

My mind carries me back to a happier time

Before you became imprisoned by your body, medication and mind.

Mother, Mother, I miss you.

She was so drugged up on prescriptions, she couldn't even comprehend what was happening. While incarcerated, they took her off her med's cold turkey. She would call me crying and begged me to come get her. I would be tough on the phone then fall apart after we ended our conversations. Weeks went by and they found her competent to stand trial. They flew her back to Salt Lake City, Utah, where I picked her up from the airport and dealt with her and her extreme withdrawals. She was found guilty and placed on four years' probation and ordered to pay restitution.

Two-ish years prior to her sentencing, I had called the bank to inquire about some shared accounts. They told me that my great grandma still needed to come in and sign some papers. I had informed them that she had been deceased for three years. The phone went silent, then they said they would need to call me back. Come to find out, things unusually fell through all the cracks, and her social security checks never stopped. My mom kept spending the money. It was put in the local paper, so it is not like I am letting the cat out of the bag, unlike the several dead kittens we pulled from her freezer. I tried to step in and manage things because I had not yet figured out that my mom was not manageable.

The entire four years of her probation were very stressful for me. Mom was on a limited disability income. I tried to help stretch her funding for the essentials; however, allocated funds would require reallocation for shoplifting and overspending. We ended up moving her into my downstairs as her home became unlivable.

My brother was living in Ogden, Utah, at the time, and Mom stayed with him for a few weeks to give my family a break. Michael moved in and out of the Valley, wherever his employment would take him. It was a good thing for him, however, with Mom divorced, my sister deceased, and him gone, the burden fell to me, Scott, and the kids. Mom's short stay with my brother was very enlightening for all of us.

Michael would call to verify Mom's stories she was spinning. She told him many lies including that I was keeping her locked in my basement and I was stealing her money. Michael, Mom, and I had a family meeting in order to straighten things out. It was the first time I had ever witnessed her backstabbing, lies, and vindictiveness firsthand. I was surprised and taken back by her callous behavior. I felt everything that I had been trying to do was for nothing. I cared more about her than she did. I mistakenly believed that if I helped her, she would get better, but I finally figured out that I was wrong.

I required therapy in order to fire myself from being HER mother as our roles had gotten tangled. From a very young age, I was conditioned to take care of my mother and her well-being. It became my job to make her feel needed and provide her with purpose. I was no longer up to the task. I did not remove her from my life entirely, but we started to play by new rules, *my* rules, with expectations and boundaries. I needed my life back. I was exhausted and wanted to conserve my energy for my own family. I prayed for guidance to help me navigate my way through. I suspected my mother of more harm than I ever knew possible. However, it was easier to accept her denials and count myself as crazy than to embrace the truth.

I pulled away from her and drew closer to my husband. I wanted to change some of my beliefs and behaviors for the better. It never crossed my mind to question them before. I had to pick through the pieces and keep what worked and let go of the rest. I went through a handful of years feeling very unsteady. I received encouragement and implemented new beliefs from my husband and his parents, gospel principles, revelation, and the power of Jesus Christ; all of which increased my testimony. It took a while, but during that time, I learned to trust Heavenly Father, my Savior, a few close friends and family members, and Scott, he was always solid. They all let me lean on them or they carried me until I regained my strength and my footing. Although I am still wobbly at times, it is not due to the principals on which I stand. I have doubts and fears, but I stabilize much faster and try not to let others shake me, not even my mother. Although, it is easier said than done.

I grasped how influential a mother is for good or evil and how her own wellness can directly affect her children. I was messed up, and I struggled with my own physical and mental health issues, but I never intentionally tried to harm my kids physically or otherwise. I never lied to them, stabbed them in the back, or tried to sabotage their life. When harmful thoughts pushed their way into my mind, I shooed them away. I know some mothers lack the ability to cast out such thoughts and succumb to the voices in their heads, I have such a mother. I tried to understand her. I wrote a paper on her for my psychology class and sympathized with her challenging circumstances. I told myself that I understand why she is the way she is. I reasoned that she was a result of her abuse and conditions, and God knew her degree of difficulty. I love her and forgive her and try to show her grace. I honestly believe that the majority of people do the best they can with what they have, this includes my mother. Most of us do not wake up and ask, how can I ruin my life, or my children's life's, or my family's life today. Yet, how often do we get the very result we try so hard to avoid.

CHAPTER FIFTEEN

Broken

*I*N MAY OF 2008 as I sat in the college auditorium in my red cap and gown, I contemplated how far I had come. My husband, children, my mom, in-laws, and my dad and his parents were in attendance to show their love and support. I wanted my kids to see that you can change direction and make new paths to fulfill your goals. I had worked hard, and everyone pitched in to help me. Prior to the Spirit nudging me in that direction I never aspired to go. I love the beauty in change, if we embrace it, we can alter our course and direction. I was proud of my accomplishment and welcomed the new scenery along this path. I had a hybrid experience with both online and in-person classes. In school, I was honing my reading, writing, and math skills. Outside of school, I was working on unlearning and relearning my life. I concluded that it is much easier to do it right the first time, but I did not get to select that option.

It is advised that the ideal is to do things in their proper order. However, many of us are not living the ideal. In a talk on CD by Jack R. Christianson, he explains that although yes, there is one standard, everyone has a different condition. As a result, the Lord tailors His mercies for His children depending on their conditions. *~ Jack R. Christianson.*

God knows what our conditions are, and they will be considered, as well as our degree of difficulty, when we are weighed and measured. At this time in my life, I was still trying to fix all of the out of order things I had done by attempting to do everything with exactness. Not only was that not possible, but it was also not until later that I learned it was unnecessary. So, there I was breaking my back to do everything just right.

After getting my associate's degree, we enjoyed the summer as a family without homework for any of us. Once school was again in session for my kids, I started subbing on and off in the schools. It was a great fit for our situation at the time. The flexible schedule and ability to accept or decline allowed me to still accomplish the several demands placed upon me. The plumbing issues we thought we left behind at our old trailer managed to find us. We had and still have several Aspen trees in our yard. The roots from those trees found their way to the cast iron plumbing pinhole leak and pushed their way through and had been growing in our pipes. Our tubs, sinks, and toilets would not drain. We cleaned and snaked them continuously.

We discovered the roots after our house flooded and ruined the flooring and the sheetrock. We emptied the contents of our food room and stacked it in the family room; to get to the plumbing, we tore out the cabinets and shelving. We had to dig up the septic tank and cut a trench through the middle of our basement foundation in order to rip out the broken, rusty pipes and replace them. The sink and toilet were removed leaving us with one bathroom for a family of seven. Scott improvised and put the toilet right over the exposed septic tank opening in the middle of the backyard.

The house was discombobulated, and I was stressed and out of sorts. At the time, my youngest daughter did not understand why I did not want her to have her birthday party at the house. She did not share my stress and was upset with me. Scott never stressed; he was great as usual. He would drill into my head that every day was a good day, and even if we were in crap up to our neck, at least it wasn't in our eyes. It was his way of reminding me that things could always be worse. I tried to look for the good in it and focus on the new carpet we would be getting and taking our old kitchen cupboards and putting them in the food room and getting used cabinets in the kitchen. We rearranged the layout in the updated kitchen and put in new countertops. It turned out more functional for our family.

I had been serving in church for achievement days but was released and called as an advisor in the young women's program again. I remember judging the president and thinking, *that's not how I would do it.*

Be careful how you criticize others because God can hear you. After camp in 2010, I was called to be the Young Women's president. I taught lessons using the correct principals, but from my perspective. My counselors and I planned and carried out events and activities, although we did not always see eye to eye. Some wanted to chase the girls that did not want to be there. Although I thought it was necessary and important, I wanted to spend more of our time and efforts on the girls that were already showing up. I would ask them to consider, "Just because they are coming does not mean that they are okay." I knew that to be true because even I was not okay at that time.

During my service as a young woman's president, I slipped and fell on the ice and performed a scorpion over the handlebars of a snowmobile, both on the same day. Those injuries caused three bulged disks and a tear in my lower back and issues in my neck. I could not get in and out of bed on my own; everyone helped me as I tried to recover. The kids had to start doing their own laundry and carried out all of the chores around the house. With doctors, chiropractors, and injections in my back and neck, they both improved over a long period of time. However, I was having other strange symptoms in addition to the neck and back.

I started itching all over the surface of my body and deep into my bones. Oversized imaginary bugs were crawling all over me. Sometimes it was like an elephant was sitting on my torso, and other times it was as if my body was filled with concrete and I could not lift my limbs. My joints felt like they were slowly being burrowed out with a hand crank drill or a melon baller. It caused me great pain to touch my skin with anything, including the water that pelted me in the shower. All things were irritating and annoying, and I had very little tolerance; literally everything was setting off my nerves. I would have the sensation of being randomly stabbed with an electric icepick, followed by tingling streamers that filtered out from the point of impact.

I was going crazy.

I was exhausted and spent much of my time in bed with the nutso symptoms and my back. I was doing the bare minimum at home and dragging myself to the temple, church, the Young Women activities, and many of my kids' events. It was all I could do to put on a brave face and pretend that I was okay. I started having suicidal thoughts and wishing that I would not wake up. Those ideas scared me, and I did not want people to find out. It was like playing pinball—the thought would force its way in, and I would try to keep it from falling out in word or action. The effort put forth in frantically hitting the flippers was exhausting. I did not realize that doing so kept the thoughts in play. They would bounce around my mind with speed and momentum, hitting every target; telling me that I was not good enough, that my family deserved a better wife and mother, and that I was completely broken and would never get well.

The problem is suicidal thoughts are not a game; it is not one you can try to outwit and win with your own skill. If one thought drained, there were more lined up waiting to be launched into play. I finally took my hands off the paddle controls and decided I needed to get help and tell my husband. He was taken back at our discussion and my request for him to lock up the hand guns.

He said, "You can't talk like that."

"If I can't tell you and let them come out of my mouth, the thoughts are going to keep bouncing around in my head. I do not want to entertain them. I need to let them go."

We made an agreement that I would share those thoughts with him right away, and even though it was hard for him, he would listen. He understood that although I never intended to act, we needed to be vigilant. I sought professional help from doctors, therapy, and divine assistance through reading, prayer, God, my Father, and His son Jesus Christ, my brother, Savior, and physician. I was led to doctors that diagnosed me with chronic fatigue, fibromyalgia, and depression. The identified conditions helped me understand what I was working with, and that it was not just all in my head. My husband joked that all things considered, I was still a little crazy. He's tried to keep my sense of humor intact, although I didn't always find him funny. Eventually, those diagnoses led to another increase in my VA disability. It helped us out financially as I was not capable of maintaining employment in my condition.

I found scriptures and conference addresses that encouraged me to keep going. Two of my favorites were both from Elder Holland, "Like a Broken Vessel" and "Broken Things to Mend," I highly recommend them. I have read them each many times. I needed constant reminders of the following:

"Whatever your struggle, my brothers and sisters—mental or emotional or physical or otherwise—do not vote against the preciousness of life by ending it! Trust in God. Hold on in His love. Know that one day the dawn will break brightly and all shadows of mortality will flee. Though we may feel we are 'like a broken vessel,' as the Psalmist says, we must remember, that vessel is in the hands of the divine potter. Broken minds can be healed just the way broken bones and broken hearts are healed." and "If you are lonely, please know you can find comfort. If you are discouraged, please know you can find hope. If you are poor in spirit, please know you can be strengthened. If you feel you are broken, please know you can be mended." ~ *Elder Jeffrey R. Holland of the Quorum of the Twelve Apostles of The Church of Jesus Christ of Latter-day Saints.*

The power of Christ's atonement helped mend me, although I was not fully healed. Consequently, through that process, I became intimately acquainted with my Savior. I can now testify with Elder Holland that, "The Savior's Atonement lifts from us not only the burden of our sins but also the burden of our disappointments and sorrows, our heartaches and our despair. When He says to the poor in spirit, 'Come unto me,' He means He knows the way out and He knows the way up. He knows it because He has walked it. He knows the way because He is the way." ~ *Elder Jeffrey R. Holland of the Quorum of the Twelve Apostles of The Church of Jesus Christ of Latter-day Saints.*

CHAPTER SIXTEEN

Angels Among Us

ℂONSTANT PRAYER helped me draw and stay close to my
father in heaven, as He was the only one perfectly aware
of my degree of difficulties. I pleaded and I begged for relief
and healing. Although it did not come how I had hoped, I was
being made spiritually whole with the aid of angelic beings on
both sides of the veil. God had sent many angels to assist me
throughout my life. I did not always acknowledge His divine
hand at the time; Susan was one exception. I had always recognized her halo. Some people believe in coincidences. Not
me. I believe in perfectly orchestrated details in our lives by a
supreme creator who loves us all. "God notices us, he watches
over us, but it is usually through others that He meets our
needs." ~ *Spencer W. Kimball former President of The Church
of Jesus Christ of Latter-day Saints.*

In 2011, our stake planned and carried out its first youth
Trek. It's a time when young adults and leaders dress like pioneers and walk while pulling handcarts and camping out. The
idea is to reenact the pioneers crossing the plains in the 1800s.
As the young women president in our ward, I wanted to participate. To get ready with my injured back, I would walk up the

side of the road and hill by our house to get in shape and break in my new hiking boots. After a discussion with Scott and very little convincing, he agreed to participate with me. While on the Trek, the kids would call us Ma and Pa. With four out of our five children attending, it was almost an entire family affair. Spring was not old enough to attend and still believes that she got hosed because she had to stay behind.

I was very nervous about my back as just walking made me swell. I was worried about sleeping on the rocky, uneven ground, and my several conditions flaring up. Because of my bladder and irritable bowel, I was concerned about the bathroom arrangements. But I was certain that Heavenly Father would help me, if I had faith. With the aid of blessings and temple trips, I kept planning and preparing.

Scott said he would show up and do it, if I would take care of all the preparations. With inspiration, I chose a name for our Trek family. It was "Rock Solid" as my husband had always been. Also, because of Scott's upbringing and activity in the church as a youth, Helaman 5:12 from The Book of Mormon was the one scripture he had remembered. I prayed Scott would have a change of heart as a result of us being there.

I was looking forward to the women's hike where they would separate the men from the family, as if they were going to war. I was hopeful that he would miss me and realize how much he needed me and the church in his life. Instead, I cried like a baby, that was not unusual. What was is the realization that I relied on my husband for absolutely everything; physical, mental, emotional, everything except for my spiritual well-being. That was the only thing he was incapable of doing for me.

The Trek theme was "Angels Among Us." We were each asked to pick an angel to help us through what was designed to be a testimony-building experience. It was for me, and of course, my angel was my sister. Scott chose his friend Charlie, Saxen had my great-grandma Marell, Skyler picked my uncle Michael Dee, JoDee got grandpa Virg, and Trigger used grandma Sue. We had several angels helping us from the other side, consistently, not just for Trek. The committee coordinated living angels from the stake, all dressed in white, to line the trail then step in to assist us with pulling our carts. It was symbolic and beautiful. I had a miraculous physical and spiritual experience. Scott was the same, he was uncomfortable with all of the feelings and expressions of love from random members; he did not run home and start going to church like I had dreamed he would.

Trek was just a small indication of the mental and physical preparation that I would need for my next significant adventure. For the 2013 hunting season, I drew a mountain goat tag. My husband insists that we put in for tags every year, as he is an avid hunter. That particular tag is luck of the draw; it is not based on points. Every year we have the same chance as everyone else, which is slim, and I didn't get my hopes up. Scott expects to draw every year and is always disappointed. That year I was scared.

In the past I had shot a cow elk, several antelope, and a few deer but nothing like this. Goats live up high, and you have to hike to get to them. Having all of my health issues it was hard to maintain regular exercise, regular anything for that matter; I never knew if or when my body would not let me out of bed. I started walking as regularly as I could and breaking in my new hunting boots. I had many of the same concerns that I had for the Trek, and I built up my stamina riding the horse.

I had helped with my friend Sharity's daughter's wedding,

and as a thank you, they gave me a Cabela's gift card. I used it to get a lightweight comfortable backpack and matching camo outfit for my hunt. If I was going to work my butt off, I wanted to match and look good doing it.

Several others expressed a desire to accompany us on the trip, but when it came down to it, only me, my husband, and father-in-law Allen were there. We saw a handful of goats and went up the steep mountain after them, with no luck. It snowed for several days. Do you know how hard it is to see a white goat in a snowstorm? On Sunday, Scott was frustrated that I would not hunt. I needed rest and was trying to keep the sabbath the best I could. I was certain that God would help me if I did my part. On Monday, we found goats, and Scott and I headed up the mountain. Allen stayed at the bottom to direct us over the walkie-talkie.

It was the hardest physical thing I had done other than boot camp. It was so steep, moist, and rocky. I tried to get one sited in, but I kept sliding down the hill. We climbed further, and Scott helped me go straight up a cliff. I was hanging on by my fingertips and toenails. Scott would take my feet and place them where they needed to be for the best footing again and again, literally supporting me and pushing me to the top. It continued to be difficult for me, side hilling in the shale that kept slipping out from under my feet. I found my goat; she was lying in a grassy patch and did not know we were there. From eighty yards away, with the wind blowing, I was able to take a break and calm my breathing.

I successfully tagged her with one shot. We got over to her and took pictures. The adrenaline wore off; I looked around and wondered how I got there and how on earth I was going to get down. Well, I got down the same way I got up. With my angelic husband pushing, pulling, carrying my heavy pack, grabbing my feet and placing them at every step through the most difficult parts. He encouraged me, telling me to keep going and that he believed in me and knew I could do it. He helped me through that hunting trip like he helps me through all else. He does almost everything short of actually doing it for me. He helps carry me because Scott has invisible wings.

Another angel in my life is my friend Sharity. She is beautiful inside and out. She moved to the Valley from Rock Springs, Wyoming, and later we were assigned as visiting teaching partners (in our church we serve by visiting women in the ward to check on them). That calling started what has now been over a twenty-year friendship. We have had challenges and trials to endure individually and ones that we have shared as a result of living in a small town, walking a similar path, living in the same ward, subbing in the same school district, and applying and competing for the same jobs. However, with it all, we have worked through the difficulties and have remained close friends.

In 2014, I accepted a ten-day challenge to journal with provided prompts. The second day asked us to pick a friend and say what we loved about them and list their positive aspects. I chose Sharity, and this is what I wrote:

I love that you are a good friend, person, and daughter of God. You are honest, and you have gone through your trials with dignity and grace. You are easy to talk to, and I never feel judged. I love that you work hard at living the gospel and don't give up. I love the example you set and the hope you give to me and others. You magnify your calling as wife, mother, daughter, friend, in your callings and as an employee. You do your best. You are considerate of others, you are amazing.

My sentiments about her are as true today as they were then. She has helped me through very rough times. My mom, my health, my jobs, my marriage, my schooling, grief, and struggles. She has been there for weddings, funerals, activities, grandchildren, excitement, and disappointments, all while managing her own life. I use her example and advice as motivation to do and be better. Most of our journey together has been trying to figure out what God wants for us. We are still in the process of that never-ending quest. I know that she was sent to be an angel in my life, she has been the answer to many prayers, and she helps carry me through.

Friends are very important; they add to and share our journey. I had very few friends outside of my family, but not Scott, he had many great friends. To this day, we both know exactly who we can call, and they would come running to help, I cannot list them all here.

It was 2015, and at that time in our lives, Cory, one of Scott's best friends, had been living in Texas. Some friends had passed away and others were just busy with their lives. Both our good friends Lance and Janice, the same couple we went on our first date with, were actively involved with our family. Their girls were our kids' age, and we were at the same place in life with the guys working, Janice and I both subbing, and we were chasing and adventuring with our kids. We would hang out, eat dinner, go to activities, events, and family outings together; the guys spent a lot of time hunting, snowmobiling, and riding motorcycles. Lance was a pro racer and was up for all kinds of adventures, if Scott called him, he was in, and vice versa.

On May 17, 2015, Scott and Lance were out riding motorcycles; it was a Sunday, and I was at church. My calling at the time was a teacher in Relief Society, and it was my turn to teach. After sacrament, right before my lesson, I received a message that one of the guys had been badly injured, but they were unsure as to which one was hurt. I had to go, another sister stepped in to teach impromptu, and I went home with my youngest daughter to figure out what was going on. I had always worried that Scott would die on me, and this could be that time. It felt like forever until we received the update, but it finally came. Lance was fatally injured and passed away. I broke down sobbing for his family, for my husband that just witnessed the passing of his friend, in relief that Scott was alive, and the reality that my friend had just lost her husband.

Scott called our son to get out there, he needed him. Skyler went and helped Scott load the bikes, it was the first time Skyler had seen his dad cry. My husband is the most stable person I have ever met but this shook him. Learning about all he had to witness and experience, I felt completely helpless, and I did not know what to do. The kids and I and others were concerned about him. Our family spent time trying to support Scott, Janice, and the girls. Scott reluctantly agreed to speak at the funeral. Everyone thought he did a great job, but he said it was one of the hardest things he ever had to do.

If you were with Lance, you were going to have a good time, that was a guarantee. It didn't matter if he was mad, sad, or happy, it could change in a second, but he would always end up happy and laughing with that contagious goofy cackle that made everyone else laugh too. Lance gave Scott some good advice years prior, not all of his advice was helpful, so Scott was skeptical, but we have used this advice many times.

He said, "If you ever find yourself arguing or fighting, ask yourself, in one year is it going to matter, if not stop because it is not worth arguing or fighting over."

When Scott and I were first married, he told me that when he died, he wanted to be cremated. I hated the idea, and he said if I would not do it, he would put someone in charge who would. We had not yet received Lance's advice, but even if we had, that topic was going to matter. I asked the bishop, and he said there was nothing in the church saying you cannot be cremated, and in some places, that is the only option. I studied the scriptures and found that if you are scattered from one end of the earth to the other, not one hair on your head shall be lost. One passage in Alma chapter 40 verse 23 tells us, "The soul shall be restored to the body, and the body to the soul; yea, and every limb and joint shall be restored to its body; yea, even a hair of the head shall not be lost; but all things shall be restored to their proper and perfect frame." Over the years, I have gotten used to the idea of cremation and decided that is what I want as well.

After watching Janice and the girls and how difficult it was for them, Scott told me, you do whatever you need to do, I will be gone and the services are for the ones that are left behind. I believed that losing a child was the hardest thing, because that was my family's experience. However, I spoke with an acquaintance at the viewing; she had lost a child and said she would have never gotten through it without her husband. She thought losing a spouse would be the worst. My mom always said that if Terri would have died in a car accident, that it would have been easier, but I went visiting teaching with a sister that lost her daughter in a car wreck and that was not the case. We all have it hard, no matter how you lose a loved one, it's hard. It is not right or fair to compare our circumstances in life to others, everyone's trials are hard for them.

Lance had told Scott and others that eagles reminded him of his dad that had passed away years earlier. At the graveside for Lance, two eagles flew overhead. There were comments that it was Lance flying with his father. I love those little reminders that our loved ones are still watching over us from the other side. I know that Lance is busy watching over his own family, but he will always be remembered at our house. Our family misses him but no one more than Scott. We refer to him and share Lance stories often, especially whenever we see eagles.

Heaven has its hands full with Lance. We assume he is causing trouble and laughing with his contagious laugh. We know he is having a fun time. He would want us all to remember the good times; keep laughing and having fun as well.

Lance's last words were, "I've got to go." We know that one day we will be reunited with all of our loved ones again, but until then we shall wait. "...they that wait upon the Lord shall renew their strength; they shall mount up with wings as eagles; they shall run and not be weary; and they shall walk, and not faint." ~ *Holy Bible Isaiah 40:31.*

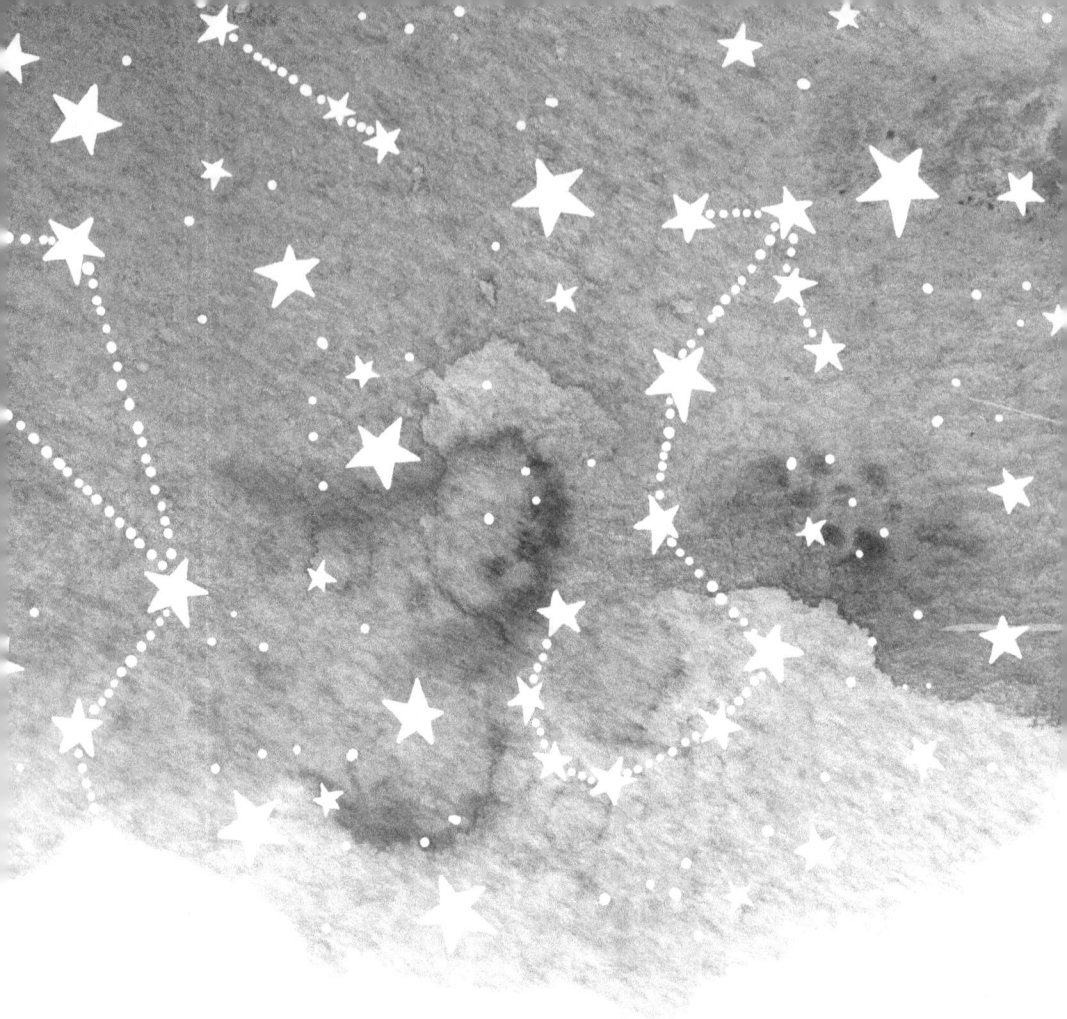

Con·ver·sion

The process of changing or causing something to change from one form to another.

CHAPTER SEVENTEEN

Change of Heart

AITING ON THE LORD IS HARD, waiting on other people is even more difficult. I know that everything is intertwined with God's timing and that we are here to learn and grow. I do not have a green thumb, but one day when I was reading The Book of Mormon, in Jacob 5 verse 47, I figured something out.

The master gardener, God, is talking about how often He has watered, tended, replanted, and "dunged" His vineyard. I was in awe, dung is fertilizer, fertilizer is crap. Gardens and God's children grow more when they are fertilized. Our trials are fertilizer to help us grow. The hard times, the crap we go through in our lives is the very dung we need in order to blossom and thrive. I now tell myself when I have a hard trial, I am being "dunged." I suppose I can laugh or cry; I usually do both.

One of several crappy situations I have had to manage in life is my relationship with my dad. It took me decades to figure out that 70 percent of what I knew about him growing up were lies my mother told me. I didn't have the truth at the time, so my thoughts and feelings were developed accordingly. I was always told that he did not love me. I thought that he left because of me, I thought because I was not a boy that he was disappointed with me. I thought… I thought… I thought wrong.

I did not get close to my dad growing up. I felt he was hard on me when he was home, but he didn't stick around either. We would have fun together, but it never lasted long. He left yearly and was in and out of our lives. My brother and I had a recent discussion, and he shared a specific memory of us three kids looking out the window crying, and Dad getting in the car and driving away. Mom was there telling us that Dad did not love us, once again as he was leaving. For all we know, he could have been driving to work. My brother and I question how many things we endured were actually true, how different our lives could have been. I know that we will not get the answers to these questions until after the resurrection.

What was true for me is how angry and hurt I was when he left us, especially the last time. What a coward I thought he was to sneak away like a thief in the night. How quickly he was able to move on. How he didn't even have the decency to keep the utilities on for us. How he wanted to spend time with his girlfriend and not his daughter. How he got remarried and forgot all about me. I did not want to go to his wedding as I thought it was disrespectful to my mother. His wife and I had words, and I called her a b***h. How my brother was welcome in their home but I was not. How Dad raised her children and gave them everything he was unwilling to give me. How they had two additional children together, and I was denied a chance to be around any of them for over twenty-five years. How I was unloved and unwanted.

When I was in high school, I was mad and preoccupied. It bothered me more that he took my blue Trans-Am, or so I told myself. I was not thinking of the long-term consequences of it all. When I was in the military, it was out of sight out of mind, mostly. He came to see my daughter briefly in the hospital after she was born, but I figured it was a good excuse for him to take a trip to California. When I moved back, he came around some, to see Saxen and me. He waited outside of the temple when I was sealed. He came and held Skyler after he was born. It started to sink in how much I had missed out on and how there was a huge hole where my dad was supposed to be.

For several years, I had a hard time with Father's Day; others would talk about their fathers and how wonderful they were and how much they had taught them. I admitted later, that due to the situation, my dad actually taught me a lot. I learned to not hold grudges. I developed tolerance, love, patience, and long suffering. I was able to encourage others to get along, apologize, and most importantly, how to forgive. Unfortunately, I had to learn the hard way, or the best way according to God. I know that He fashions our trials just for us, again with the special fertilizer.

After Scott and I got together and I knew that Lyman, Wyoming, was going to be our permanent home, I was well aware that my dad and his family were always ten minutes away. I never really ran into them much. Dad would come visit me for five or ten minutes here and there, and we would check in with each other and express how we wished things could be different. But his wife would not allow it, she had his whole family well trained. I was invited over to spend time with extended family, and other times I would be politely uninvited. If Dad's wife and their kids were there, I would not be welcome.

It was extremely painful watching my dad take care of his new family, loving them more than me. It was crushing to drive past my grandparents' house on many occasions, and their yard would be filled with vehicles from Utah, Texas, and of course, Wyoming. The whole family was there spending time together, enjoying each other's company, except me and sometimes my brother. My kids and Scott would try to console me as they had to witness my anguish and tears. Being excluded from your own family is one of the worst feelings there is. My grandma would attempt to smooth things over and make me feel better. I knew it wasn't her fault; she was just hoping to keep the peace and was doing the best she could. I tried to enjoy and maintain the relationships that were still intact even with all the boundaries and caution tape.

I was not perfect and definitely contributed to the situation. I could not undo what had been done, but I wanted to find a way for it to get better. I gave Christmas gifts that were never received and told Dad to tell her I was sorry. I hand tied polar fleece blankets for them one year, not because I am a saint, but for a peace offering and to show love. I was driving around going to yard sales one summer; just following the directions to the address I typed into the GPS. It took me to their house, I did not realize the yard sale was there, I never knew their address. Cars and people lined the street. I decided to be brave and get out. I wished I wouldn't have. I walked around the sale just for a bit before I saw the polar fleece blankets I had made, brand new, for sale, on the table.

All the years of hurt hit me, and I took the blankets and left. I am positive people saw me stealing items from her. I justified that I had already paid for them once. I felt guilty, and Dad later told me that it was a major setback. Given the situation, I did not think it was ever going to get better with his wife anyway. Dad and I continued for a few more years with visits here and there and an occasional birthday party, lunch, or dinner. I loved my dad, and as I discovered more of the truth, I apologized for not having all of the information. Dad never bad-mouthed my mom, he said he hoped one day Michael and I would figure it out on our own. During our visits, he was a trooper to set through all of my inquiries and dredging up the past, although as a result, his and my relationship was improving.

I had been taught and believed that as we strive to become more like Christ, His love changes us, and we can begin to see others as Heavenly Father does. Although we are imperfect in our abilities to comprehend the love of God for all of His children, it is our responsibility to love and forgive each other anyway, as we are all in need of forgiveness.

I forgave my dad and myself for all the misunderstandings and it felt better, but it did not fix the situation with the entire family. I started going to institute class on Tuesdays in the fall of 2016. I really enjoyed the discussions, the women, their knowledge and testimonies of the gospel. I learned a lot and my testimony grew as well. The class moved into the topic of family history. We were told of many promises offering heal-ing for families as they participate in finding and sealing their ancestors through temple work. This healing can take place both in heaven and on earth.

Although I was doing temple work, I decided I could step it up. As I increased my efforts, I began being nudged to heal things with my step mother. I knew that she and my dad loved each other and that she made him happy. I had forgiven her long ago and concluded that she had her own difficulties, but I was never provided an opportunity to let her know. I desired a more positive outcome than the one we were headed for. At the beginning of December 2016, we had an amazing institute class. Some of us stayed after and continued to visit. The topic of my sister passing away and me not being welcome in my dad's home for over two-and-a-half decades came up. I mentioned that I had been feeling the Spirit to go and try to fix it. One sister challenged me to do it that week. I knew if I went home, I would chicken out. I drove straight to their house, knowing that my dad was at work.

I thought I needed an icebreaker, so I wrote her a check for the blankets I had stolen a few years prior. I knocked on the door, very fearful of it being slammed in my face. I asked if we could speak and she shockingly invited me in. I tried to give her the check and started crying. I apologized for anything and everything that I had ever done to hurt her.

She ripped up the check and said, "I don't want your money." She apologized and told me she had been wanting to talk to me for a while. That she had been such a "B" to me, and she was sorry. We hugged, cried, and visited. It was wonderful; a huge weight had been lifted. I was there for five hours. We discussed canning, remodeling, rentals, family, and the dog.

"Forgiving ourselves and others is not easy. In fact, for most of us it requires a major change in our attitude and way of thinking—even a change of heart." ~ *President Dieter F. Uchtdorf former Second Counselor in the First Presidency of the Twelve Apostles of The Church of Jesus Christ of Latter-day Saints.*

I am not sure what changed her heart, but I am so grateful for it. Even though she and I decided that we were good, it did not magically mend things for everyone. Some of my kids were happy for me, and others decided just because I forgave her, didn't mean they had to. We still can't enjoy relationships that were never cultivated in the first place, but things are better, much better.

Dad and my stepmom built a house over in Lyman, and we discussed, although I was not welcome in their old house, that I would always be welcome in their new one. I love my dad and stepmom very much; I admire and respect them. She is one of the hardest working people that I have ever met. We actually have a lot in common. I know that we cannot get back all of those years that we lost, but we are doing great, and I want to continue being great moving forward. We have forgiven each other, and I hope one day everyone who still has hang-ups with either of us can learn to forgive also.

"Because we all depend on the mercy of God, how can we deny to others any measure of the grace we so desperately desire for ourselves? ...should we not forgive as we wish to be forgiven?" ~ *President Dieter F. Uchtdorf former Second Counselor in the First Presidency of the Twelve Apostles of The Church of Jesus Christ of Latter-day Saints.*

Another crappy case where I had to learn to implement many of the same lessons learned from the situation with my dad was with the consequences from my service in the military. An article came out in the *American Legion* magazine in January 2017, "Nothing Wrong With You."

It proceeded to describe the twenty-five-year struggle to receive acknowledgement and proper treatment for health issues. It reported thousands of veterans suffering from illnesses due to the burn pits, toxins, chemicals, pesticides, excessive vaccinations, including experimental ones, as a result of their service in the Gulf War. I am still not sure what number of the twenty some shots I received were experimental, nor was I aware of any at the time. We are still learning more and more about the side effects from the COVID vaccine, so times that by who knows how many? Add those to my time in Saudi

Arabia and off the coast of Mogadishu near the burn pits, and the five months I walked past the asbestos removal. No wonder I have "Gulf War Syndrome."

GWS "is characterized by a cluster of persistent, unexplained symptoms that can include fatigue, headaches, joint pain, muscle pain, gastrointestinal problems, respiratory issues, sleep disturbances, neurological problems, and more." ~ *Gulf War Syndrome, also known as Gulf War Illness.*

I had known that many of my health concerns were presumed to be caused or aggravated by my service, but this was the first time that I had learned that they purposely used me as a guinea pig for their experiments. I was mad, frustrated, and felt betrayed by my country. I cried and prayed to be able to forgive and let go of my hard feelings, asking God to soften my heart. It took me several years to trust going to the VA Hospital; I associated them as one and the same. I met a woman whose job was doing the billing for the VA; she convinced me to seek treatment there and assured me that they provided great services. I did start to establish my care at the VA facility in Salt Lake, and I have been fairly happy with the support and health care they offer.

I know what all of the right answers are. I know that God has a plan for me, and that everything happens for a reason, and that everything will be turned for my good. I know that my trials are for my learning and growth, and that they can draw me closer to Him if I choose to let them. I know that Jesus can heal all my pain, wounds, hurt, disappointments, sorrows, and grief. I know that I will forgive, eventually. Although sometimes the space between my questions and the answers I already have is a lot of unknowing.

CHAPTER EIGHTEEN

My Path

*B*ELIEVING THAT GOD had a plan for me, I was constantly trying to figure out what that plan was. I like to play a game where I try to outsmart God. I always lose but I still play. I look ahead and imagine all of the possible dangers and problems, and I try to fix them before they even happen. I was able to enjoy mostly being a stay-at-home mom. I had temporary, flexible jobs that allowed me to manage all of my church callings and other duties as mother, wife, daughter, veteran, and friend. It worked well, but I could foresee that it was not sustainable. In just a few short years with each child that left, I was one step closer to being out of a job.

How do you keep that job once all of your children leave? I was tired of cleaning all the time; I had done that my whole life. I found an article on the eleven ways to keep your house "clean enough," I wish I would have saved it. Why did my floor need to be clean enough to eat off of? Why are we eating off the floor? Although funny, I used cleaning as an escape and kept cycling in it. I realized I had been doing it since my sister passed away. Although I enjoy a clean home, my behaviors in that area were excessive and demanded a change. I relaxed and eased up on the obsessive cleaning, but then I would sit at home and cry and wonder what I was going to do with myself all day. Surely, I had more to offer. Certainly, God had something additional in mind for me.

I looked into continuing my education and found an expensive online program through the University of Wyoming. Where I live, options are limited. I was not passionate about that path, but I was accepted, and Scott and I agreed that education was a good investment. However, issues kept arising; money, the kids, the timing, the program—I was frustrated that things were not working out. Time moved forward as it does, and I kept an eye out for possible solutions. I continued accepting callings, serving my family, others, and subbing.

Every year, our Valley celebrates Pioneer Days at the end of July. The church wards in the stake take turns with the various assignments for the parade, BBQ, triathlon or race, flag raising ceremony, advertisements, or the talent show. I took several turns decorating the ward float. I had been put in charge of an antique, arts, quilts, and collectibles display in 2009 in lieu of the talent show that year. In 2016, I was once again called to be in charge of the talent show. This time the BYU Idaho dancers volunteered to come and perform. I was assigned the task of coordinating and securing a location, meals, housing, and working closely with the advertisement team. It was stressful but right up my alley. I liked those kinds of assignments; they align well with my skill set.

I put our home at the bottom of the list for a backup place for a pair of dancers to lodge. Scott didn't love the idea of any of them staying the night in our home but agreed if absolutely necessary. I had the food all lined out, the location secured, advertisement taken care of, and homes arranged for the dancers and chaperones. I had a long list of backup homes before it would ever get to Scott and me. As you can guess, things kept falling through with my list of housing options. Using our home became necessary. I embraced that everything happens for a reason and jokingly predicted that maybe there was a young man that was going to fall in love with one of our beautiful daughters.

Scott accompanied me for the first ten minutes; although the program was wonderful, it was not his thing. In the middle of the second routine, I looked over at him in his misery and said, "You can go. I will see you at home." I did not need to tell him twice. The performance went off without a hitch. I received several compliments for my labors. Two male dancers and I got home late. Scott was awaiting our arrival with pizza, drinks, and conversation. We visited, and the dancers told us about their traveling summer schedule and their unique college experiences at BYUI (Brigham Young University-Idaho).

A very distinct voice popped into my head and told me, "This is why they're here."

The next morning, after gathering at our church's Stake Center and sending the entire crew off on their bus with sack lunches, I was eager to go home and start looking into the BYUI programs of study. Instead, I found the new Pathway Program, an educational program through BYUI.

It was an inexpensive educational opportunity for members, and now friends, of the church to gather weekly and receive or continue their education. It was the answer to my several prayers and desire to continue my formal learning. It is my understanding that it works a bit different after COVID and other modifications, but at the time, we had to have enough local interest and request and receive approval for it to be conducted in our area.

My first step was to seek approval from the stake president. My friend Sharity's parents had been on a mission for our church; they received special permission to see one of their children off prior to that child's military reassignment overseas. That Sunday, they just happened to be in attendance in our ward and just happened to be the Pathway missionaries. Sharity's mom explained more about how it worked. The stake president happened to be available after church, and I was able to meet with him and gain his approval to move forward. Within weeks, he was released from his calling, but he encouraged me to not let it fall through the cracks.

I didn't let it, or I should say God didn't let it. It was His work, and I was just a willing tool in His hands. I recruited and went to regional meetings and recruited some more. We had a great amount of interest, so much so that they called missionaries in our area to facilitate, and when all was said and done, fourteen of us participated in the inexpensive, one-year, weekly gathering, certificate earning program. It was amazing, and I learned so much. I made new connections, Amy who became a lifelong friend, and my testimony increased exponentially. Specifically, during one class, the Spirit testified that the Pathway Program was considered to be one of the great and stirring events preparatory to the second coming. How amazing is it that to better prepare for the Savior, we can educate ourselves. I was honored to be a part of His great work.

While participating in the program, I applied for a para position at the school. During the interview, they were offering a long-term substitute teaching spot with the possibility of a para job after that. I had done several subbing assignments, and I enjoyed them, so I agreed to the grab-bag job if they needed me there. That is the position I was offered, and then

I was upset that I did not get a permanent para job. My wise daughter pointed out that it was better than no job at all. Three days before school started, I jumped in head first. I decorated the room, did the bulletin boards, lesson plans, desk arrangements, back to school night with the parents, etc. I was given the opportunity to be a teacher, and I was pretty good at it. I'm sure I was not measured with the same ruler as a real teacher would have been, but I received several compliments from parents, teachers, and staff.

I had access to employees to help with my Pathway class assignments of interviewing people in my field of interest. I researched probable educational paths for becoming a teacher; I decided that is what I wanted to do. I remember the Spirit I felt when talking to another teacher, and she advised me about upcoming opportunities. She said, "You need to keep in mind how many people will be retiring in the district in the next couple of years." I was concerned with there being an available position down the road, but I knew through the Spirit that there would be.

I was able to be a "teacher" the entire first half of the year. I conducted parent teacher conferences, graded papers, school pictures, and the Christmas concert. I did not want it to end; I loved my students. Inevitably it did end, and I came back after the holiday break as a long-term para because the permanent position had fallen through. I was good with it as I was now focused on going back to school to become a teacher. I was accepted, registered, and ready to start down that educational path. Again, it did not work out, things kept happening with my mom, and I had to postpone a few times.

Under unusual circumstances, the possibility of another long-term subbing job became available for the 2018–2019 school year, and I was impressed to apply for it. I filled out the teacher application, cover letter, resume, and four letters of recommendation. The letters definitely took the longest to round up. I did not get the job. Once again, I was frustrated and obviously was not understanding the revelation or inspiration I thought I was receiving. I kept subbing but was getting tired of it and felt stuck. It was my youngest daughter's senior year. I was enjoying what time I had left with her but still worried about what I was going to do once I was fired from my stay-at-home mom position.

A friend had asked me to write her a letter of recommendation as she was applying to be a teacher for one of the school's openings. I had gone to the website to wallow in the opportunities I was still not in a position to explore. I noticed another available spot at the district office for the PowerSchool Administrator and inquired about it but was easily deterred. Scott and I were traveling the five-hour drive home from regional basketball and discussing my options. We had just determined that I was going to get my bachelor's degree through the continuing online Pathway program. With that settled, I reclined the seat and closed my eyes for a much-needed nap.

The thought came very clear: "You need to apply for the PowerSchool job."

I argued with God in my head, "It is not a teaching job."

His answer, "If I wanted you to be a teacher, you would be on that path."

I quickly called my friend and told her that I was inspired to apply for that position. Sharity informed me that she had also applied. Feeling that she would get the job over me, I still listened to inspiration and went in Monday morning to inquire and apply. I was discouraged from applying but encouraged to apply for a different position that had not yet been posted. I concluded that the inspiration was to get me in there for the other position.

That night, again I was told to apply for the PowerSchool position. I called the next day and asked for my name to be added to that job also. The beauty is with the short timeline and me being out of town for regional and state basketball, I would not have had time to do the application or collect letters of recommendation. Because I had applied for the job at the beginning of the year, the one I did not get, my application was already on file, and they just transferred it to the new openings I was interested in. Thank you, Heavenly Father. To make an extremely long story shorter, God moved mountains for me. I ended up finally being offered and accepted that job. All of the inspiration I had received came together, and I understood in a profound way that what is meant for you will not pass you by, and that God will not let you get very far in the wrong direction.

After starting my new job, I learned more and more about the smallest details of what took place. I knew that God was involved every step of the way. In my patriarchal blessing, there is a promise that as I interact with coworkers and have their eternal interest in mind, that I can develop charity and love for them. One day I was at work, I had not been there very long when I was told, "These are the coworkers I was talking about." Regardless of all that transpired, that job was always meant to be mine.

Because I had received such strong inspiration to continue my education, I kept trying to take classes. It was difficult to work ten hours a day, learn my new job, and do school work. The last thing I wanted to do was be on the computer all day, then go home and get on the computer some more. Every fourteen weeks I was stressing out about what classes I should take. Finally, after deciding I could not keep up, I would need to drop the class(s). I knew that schooling was a good thing, but my goal of obtaining an education was to secure a good job, and I had accomplished that.

I prayed again and again to understand what Heavenly Father needed me to do. I received a blessing that it was time for me to enjoy my life. I decided to let go of my formal education and unenrolled from school completely so that I would not torture myself every term. I found a quote that described my condition perfectly:

"If we have received personal revelation for our situation and the circumstances have not changed, God has already answered our question." ~ *Elder Dale G. Renlund of the Quorum of the Twelve Apostles of The Church of Jesus Christ of Latter-day Saints.*

My circumstances had changed, dramatically since I had originally received revelation about my schooling. Once my situation had changed, it was appropriate that that specific inspiration no longer applied.

Along those same lines I love the saying, "You cannot solve today's problems with yesterday's solutions." ~ *Unknown*

I have found this to be true on more than one occasion. As our lives and circumstances change, we must learn to adapt and change with them.

〜

CHAPTER NINETEEN

Trust Him

I HAD BEEN LOOKING FORWARD to turning fifty for several years. A fiftieth birthday is a big deal, and I was excited. I know people who dread getting older but not me. With my sister passing away at fifteen, she did not get a chance to age. I feel aging is a privilege not all people get to experience. I was so excited for my birthday and wanted a special party, but it did not go as I hoped. I'm not complaining, it was good. More than anything, I wanted my husband there. However, he arranged for all of my girls to go out to eat with me and go back to the house and have dessert and visit while he went hunting in search of a big deer that he did not end up with. The eve of my birthday, after everyone left, I turned on the music and I danced.

On September 1, 2023, my birthday month started with the death of my Aunt Rena, my mom's baby sister. When loved ones pass away, it can cause some reflection. Between that and reaching a half century of life, I actively reached out to my Heavenly Father for guidance on how I should spend my fiftieth year and what He wanted me to focus on. I prayerfully consulted a clean copy of my patriarchal blessing. I felt the

Spirit so strong when I read the part, "Blessed are those who put their trust in the Lord." I had no idea what I was in for, but I knew that I would need to heavily rely on and trust in God to do it.

Not even a month later in mid-October, it started. I had been working at my job for almost five years. The position I was hired for was inspired, and God moved mountains for me to get it. However, I had been advocating for some changes at work as I did not agree that the schedule aligned with the required job duties. After the front desk employee got her dream job mid-year and left a vacancy in the district office, higher-ups conspired a plan. I was informed of the new arrangement.

The plan was for me to continue working my full-time job and to "absorb" the front desk position as well. My boss changed; my pay would be split funded from two different departments, and I would go from a ten-month employee to a year-round employee; that was the only part I had been advocating for. My new boss threatened that if I was unwilling to do both jobs that I would not have a job at all. I negotiated an hourly raise that was later revoked. My pay did go up a bit because of the additional days added to my contract. I felt peace and calm while hearing the plan and knew that this was one of the things that I was going to need to trust the Lord with. I told my new supervisor that I would discuss it with my husband: although, I was going to say yes, what choice did I have? I agreed to the changes and through tears, tried to put on a brave face, and sent out a positive email to staff.

I was so stressed and overwhelmed. I could not sleep and that added to my already emotional state. When I was hired, I was 80 percent disabled through the VA and continuously dealing with my ongoing chronic health issues. Stress and no sleep negatively impacted my immune system. My sinus issues were triggered, and as a result, I had to schedule my third sinus surgery in November. Days prior to that surgery, I was at the VA for a doctor's appointment. It was the first time ever hearing about the recently passed Pact Act, a law that expands VA Health Care and benefits for Veterans exposed to burn pits, Agent Orange, and other toxic substances.

They had so many questions about my exposure in the Navy. I started to uncontrollably ugly cry. I was so upset with the government, with my job, and with others forcing their agendas on me. Everything came together at that moment and hit me like a freight train.

My primary care doctor was taken back by my fragile state. She said, "I have been seeing you for years, and I have never seen you like this."

I replied, "I am a hot mess."

She corrected me, "Let's be clear, you are a *high functioning hot mess.*"

I joke that it is my official diagnosis.

She could not allow me to leave in my condition without calling in the mental health team. I was seen and scheduled for follow-up visits. All of those visits led to other appointments. My sinus surgery went well. However, I started snoring afterward and had a hard time swallowing. With my IBS, I had a colonoscopy scheduled in March, and they added an upper scope to see what was going on. They found and removed a 3mm or 1 ½ inch precancerous adenoma and found three ulcers. I was prescribed medicine for the ulcers and another colonoscopy in six weeks to make sure they removed all of the adenoma with good margins. It was a long six weeks. I ended up with a staph infection. My tongue was swelling up so large at night that it would wake me up gagging me and cutting off my air. That led to CT neck scans, bloodwork, sleep studies, and another upper scope added to the upcoming colonoscopy. My bloodwork was fine as always, CT scan clear, upper scope resulted in my throat needing to be stretched so much that I had to go on a two-day soft diet when it did not even require stretching just six weeks prior. They learned the entire adenoma had been removed but found an additional polyp. It was either missed the first time, or it grew in six weeks; either way, not good.

My severe neck, shoulder, and arm pain was increasing. They had previously ruled out nerve damage and carpal tunnel. X-rays and MRIs on my neck and shoulder revealed old injuries and wear and tear but nothing significant enough to explain my pain. My toes were going numb. My eye pain and ocular migraines were at an all-time high. My eye doctor suspected diabetes, so we went down that rabbit hole. Turns out that I was not diabetic but was prescribed the maximum dose of metformin; I declined it. A different eye doctor diagnosed severe dry eye and prescribed aggressive treatment of migraines suggesting Botox injections. My new doctor at the VA called me at the end of July and informed me that he suspected I could have MS. I had never considered MS, but I agreed to rule it in or out. It made sense with my various symptoms. I was having brain fog and forgetting things. My motor skills were affected, and I was struggling to type and coordinate my brain and hands. While driving, I was aware that I was confused, all this in addition to my usual issues.

My husband continued driving me everywhere except for work. He took me to all of my appointments and would wait for hours while I was getting MRIs of my brain or lumbar spine. He was there for my spinal tap and drove me back to the ER with a probable leak from the procedure. It was the first time in twenty-seven years of marriage that my husband did not hunt and stayed home because of me.

I said, "You missed my fiftieth birthday, and that was important to me—why stay home now?"

He said, "Because you're a mess."

We both knew that I had been a mess on several other occasions. "I've been a mess before."

"Never like this."

He was worried about me and was not going to leave. I appreciated it as I did not want to be alone. I started having suicidal thoughts again, and although determined to keep shooing them away, my strength was compromised.

After almost a year of what felt like nothing but work, stress, and going to doctors, I prayerfully revisited my patriarchal blessing. I read it on my sister's birthday seeking additional guidance and direction. Once again, the Spirit let me know that I would need to continue to trust Him. In addition to that revelation, Heavenly Father finally answered a longtime question concerning another statement in my blessing. Over the years, I had read and reread and prayed and wondered; if Scott was the man that God had prepared JUST FOR ME. The man who my love for him and his love for me would only be exceeded by our individual love for the Lord. The power of the Spirit was so strong in letting me know that Scott was THE ONE. He was prepared just for me. He loved me more than anything, except God; another revelation, my husband loved God. It was like getting run over by a second train, except this time, instead of being overwhelmed with hurt and frustration, I was overpowered with love and joy.

I decided that if the only perk to everything I was going through was to gain a testimony of my husband's deep love for me and Heavenly Father, it was all worth it. Yet, I knew God had more in store for me, and this particular journey was not over. In light of the Pact Act covering issues that were not previously acknowledged as presumptive, I started the paperwork to increase my disability. I had been diagnosed long ago with conditions now considered to be caused or aggravated by my military service. I was in the right place at the right time, all documented to prove location and exposure. It took time but resulted in my disability going up another 10 percent. I decided to start an additional claim to up my ratings for three other service-connected disabilities. Regardless of the MS diagnosis, the severity of my existing conditions were enough to justify an increase on their own.

I found out right before Christmas that I did not have MS. On one hand, it was a relief, I did not want MS. On the other hand, it was frustrating as I still did not have the answers or validation I was looking for. It is hard to accept that an invisible disease can cause so much damage. Knowledge about fibromyalgia has come a long way since my original diagnosis. At least now it is considered a real disorder, with its own code and everything. Still, some do not consider it creditable; I was even on that list for years and I had it. It is a neurological disease that makes you think you are crazy and question everything you feel. You learn that you can't trust yourself or your body as it actively tries to sabotage you. It affects your thoughts, mood, behavior, movement, and motivation. It slowly chips away your quality of life and your ability to function.

It had already been decided that I needed to make changes at work. I could not keep operating in the elevated fight or flight mode. I tried to handle everything they threw my way. I was managing the workload, but the two jobs were not conducive. I maintained two offices with two completely different types of work. One type of work demanded active involvement and interactions with the workings of the district. The other type needed privacy, quiet time, and space to code, review, and compare data, and discuss confidential student information. If I was doing one job, the other was not getting done. Every day I was torn. Because the front was more like constantly putting out fires, it left the job I was hired to do unattended on the back burner. I seemed to be the only one worried about it boiling over or evaporating all together.

After receiving a work email forcing more time out front, I was done. I had been constantly pushing myself to stay in flight, and my tank was already on reserve. If I did not land immediately, I was going to crash and burn. I was prepared to quit my job entirely. My husband agreed; it didn't seem necessary to keep a job or have retirement if it was going to put me in the ground. I requested a priesthood blessing as I always do in my important decision-making process. Over the weekend, I thoughtfully and prayerfully composed a letter in response to the email. It was received with an urgent response for a face-to-face conversation; it went very well. I told them what I was going through, as they were unaware. I actually felt heard for the first time in six years. They were intrigued with my not all or nothing proposal as demanded when the arrangement started. I proposed a divinely inspired compromise to cut back to part-time and give up a chunk of money and my medical benefits. It took a few months to even approve and then work out all of the details. I was able to start my new reduced days and hours doing one job, my job, at the beginning of the new year.

I received a call in mid-January from a VA claims employee. She informed me that I had filed the wrong paperwork. She told me exactly what paperwork I needed and shared additional forms my doctor could fill out that would speed up the process. She made a point to let me know that if this would have come across any other desk, it would have been stamped, denied, and thrown in a pile, requiring me to start all over. Later, the claims department reached out again. This time to set up appointments with contracted third parties as part of their decision-making process. My address would not populate nearby providers, and after several attempts, they decided to use the local post office address; this was commonly done in cases like mine. After locating and scheduling with providers, I was told they would FedEx me all of the paperwork detailing times and instructions. Two days before my first appointment, a delivery woman was shown to my office at work. She tried to deliver the package to the post office, the address they used for me, but the post office would not accept it. She was going to return it but then realized that she recognized my name and remembered that I worked at the district office. I showed my gratitude for her willingness to go above and beyond. Both times I acknowledged divine intervention on my behalf.

I stressed about the appointments and expressed my frustration with the required steps. I worried how I was going to convey the severity of my issues to someone I had never met before in less than one hour? I prayed and put it in God's hands. He had gotten me this far; I was willing to walk with Him further. I gave it a few weeks after the completion of all my appointments, but no status change. By the end of February, I was even more curious about where the VA was at in the process. I logged into the system, and they had created and mailed a letter on Valentine's Day, another reminder that God loved me. I had not received it by mail but was able to click on it and read it. I was overcome with emotion and relief when I learned that I had been awarded 100 percent disability.

The money that I had to give up by cutting back at work was made up for with the increase. I am so blessed, but more than the money, I wanted—NO, *I needed* the validation that my struggles were real. I needed acknowledgement of what I had experienced in my life and how my service caused or exacerbated my issues. Also, that my quality of life and my ability to work and handle stress had been negatively impacted by them. It took me a bit to work out some hard feelings, and I do not completely blame the district or the parties involved. The situation aggravated my pre-existing conditions; it did not cause them. No one on earth had any way of knowing that my body would react to the added stress as it did, including me.

CHAPTER TWENTY

Just Breathe

*G*OING THROUGH MY RECENT TRIAL helped me draw even closer to God, the Father and His son, Jesus Christ, both male, eternal beings with glorified bodies of flesh and bone. Through the Holy Ghost, a spirit, and the third member of the divine Godhead, I have been guided and directed along my path. I believe that they are three distinct personages with one purpose. I interchange and call the members of the Godhead by their many recognizable names. Regardless of what name I use to address the three of them, the source is the same. Their purpose is the same, to bring us, God's children, back home.

"This is my work and my glory—to bring to pass the immortality and eternal life of man." ~ *Pearl of Great Price Moses 1:39.*

Sometimes when I ponder immortality I think, I'm not sure if I want to live forever, not in my current condition anyway. I am excited to receive my resurrected, perfect body. My physical health is fair on most days and poor on the others, although you would never know my condition just by looking at me. I continue to struggle with my mental health, but it is better than it used to be, and I am getting faster at pulling out of a dark hole or avoiding the abyss altogether. I now have more tools at my disposal than I did before. All of those appointments at the VA that lead to even more appointments; some of them were from their Whole Health initiative. ~ *Whole Health centers around what matters to you, not what is the matter with you.*

Using this approach, I gained understanding for my chronic pain management through specific therapy. I started pacing my activities as opposed to all or nothing. I put some hobbies back into my life I was still capable of doing, like writing. I started grounding, and I stopped focusing on all the things that I couldn't do anymore and started enjoying the ones I could. I better understood the logistics of chronic conditions and stopped beating myself up for them. I accepted my diagnosis and the answers I already had. Through biofeedback, I had learned that I was not breathing.

Well, obviously I was breathing, but I was not breathing well. I was stuck in fight or flight mode, and everything about my short rapid breaths and heartbeat was sending signals to my body that we were in danger. I didn't realize how long I had been holding my breath. Anticipating my mother's mood; waiting for my dad to leave; my husband to quit drinking; Skyler to get up; someone to die, leave, or stop loving me. I stayed still and held my breath to keep from jarring my back and neck, to hold my body tight to help control the pain. I literally had a pulmonary function test performed previously because I could not get enough air. I had not been using my lungs fully for so long, my lung capacity diminished. Our bodies are amazing at adapting to trauma, injury, or pain to keep us safe, but sometimes we get stuck there.

Most times, the people around us at work, church, our extended family and friends don't know all of the things that we are dealing with; they will not know unless we tell them. I believe it is one of the many tools Satan uses to keep us weighed down. We think that we can't share with others, or that we need to handle it, or that we can manage everything ourselves. We try to deal with personal and family issues internally to avoid judgment or embarrassment. I know that for years I put a smile on my face and pushed through at school, in public, at work, or church so that everyone would think I was fine. I don't do that anymore. I no longer want to spend that much time and energy pretending that I am okay. I need that energy elsewhere.

I try to be selective; I don't want to be the person across the counter that spills my life story on you when you ask how my day is. I now respond with, "how much time do you have, do you really want to know, are you just being nice?" If I don't know you well, my answer will still be I am doing good, unless you catch me on a bad day, and then I just might spill. I believe that we need to put a smile on our face and push through what we can. Not all things are tragic or the end of the world, as we can make them out to be, but some things are. More importantly, we need to learn to recognize the difference and when to reach out for help. God does not intend for us to do everything on our own.

Like many men and women I know, I do not like to ask for assistance. I got caught up in staying busy and distracted, I functioned that way for years, still doing good things. It kept my mind occupied and that allowed me to ignore my problems, my body, all of the pain, and unfortunately, other people. I limited my activities and interactions because, like my lungs, I did not have the capacity to deal with everything, or everyone. I have learned that ignoring problems does not make them go away. Shoving things down or putting them to the side does not fix them, it fills us up and, as a result, pushes on vital organs limiting our capacity to fully live and breathe. Issues will come back sooner or later and will insist on being addressed.

My later is now.

I wonder when my brother's time will be, when all of his unresolved trauma will demand his attention. He and I have been conversing more recently, going through and validating our memories. He was on the receiving end of many of the same difficulties I was growing up. He lost his sister too. After I moved out, graduated, and went to the military, he was left behind. Michael told me he felt abandoned by me as well. Plus, he has had his own journey and trials that he has had to endure—that is his story to tell, and I am only aware of a small portion of his many struggles. I love my brother and his family very much.

Michael and I stayed in touch over the years, but I wouldn't say that we are extremely close. After comparing notes, we think our mother had a lot to do with that. She would falsely tell me things about him and him things about me that created distance between us. Our mother has helped us both out in times of need, and we love her; she is our mother. However, she is both the hero and the villain in our stories. We find it ironic that our unstable mother was our stability. We cannot change the past; we can only try to do and be better moving forward. The issue is that how we have developed and choices we have made, were because of what happened, as a result of the misinformation we both believed. It is pointless to ponder

how things could have been different because they are not;
although, I have wasted time doing just that. This is the life
we were given to work with, and Michael and I both try to
improve and make the best of what we have been given. It has
never been a competition, but we have definitely taken turns
being on the high or low end of the teeter-totter. It would be
nice if we could help each other achieve more balance; we are
working on that.

When I had the opportunity to fill in as a teacher, I learned
a magic word. That word is YET; it brings hope. When we say
I can't do that, or *I don't understand*, it lacks room for growth
and progress, it limits us. But if we say, *I can't do that yet*, or
I don't understand that yet, it creates space between where we
are and where we want to be. *Yet* gives us time to figure it out,
time to learn. It took me a long time, and I wish everyone
understood that God looks at sin and weakness differently,
that we are strengthened through grace and that the Savior's
atonement is the ultimate act of God's love. I wish for everyone
to know and feel that they are loved. That our worth is not
determined by our actions, and there is nothing we can do
to lessen our value in the eyes of God, we have already been
purchased and paid for.

As Elder Hirst said there is a difference between being loved
and feeling loved. "...Perhaps you feel a long way from the
love of God. Maybe there is a chorus of voices of discouragement and darkness that weighs into your thoughts, messages
telling you that you are too wounded and confused, too weak
and overlooked, too different or disoriented to warrant heavenly love in any real way. If you hear those ideas, then please
hear this: those voices are just wrong." He continues, "You
might know something secret about yourself that makes you

feel unlovable. However right you might be about what you know about yourself, you are wrong to think that you have put yourself beyond the reach of God's love." ~ *Elder Karl D. Hirst of the Quorum of Seventy of The Church of Jesus Christ of Latter-day Saints.*

I spent several years being wrong, thinking that I was unloved, not allowing myself to accept God's love, or the genuine love of others. I was keeping all of my secrets, holding my breath so no one would find out about them as well as hiding from the Lord. He already knew them, and He loved me anyway; I just couldn't feel it.

If "you are wrestling with grief, depression, betrayal, loneliness, disappointment, or other powerful intrusion into your ability to feel God's love for you...perhaps you will not be able to feel His love...[YET]" ~ *Elder Karl D. Hirst of the Quorum of Seventy of The Church of Jesus Christ of Latter-day Saints.*

I recently found a podcast where they discussed that sometimes the words we use are limiting, such as "feeling" the Spirit. It can hinder our ability to recognize the several ways we can experience the Spirit. The Holy Ghost is heart and mind, suggesting that we not only feel the Spirit but we can have cognitive spiritual thoughts, ideas, dreams, enlightenment and the ability to know and believe on the words of others. ~ *Gospel Chats Podcast Episode Ten.*

So please believe Elder Holland when he tells you, "...however late you think you are, however many chances you think you have missed, however many mistakes you feel you have made or talents you think you don't have, or however far from home and family and God, you feel you have traveled, I testify that you have not traveled beyond the reach of divine love. It is not possible for you to sink lower than the infinite light of

Christ's Atonement shines." ~ *Elder Jeffrey R. Holland of the Quorum of the Twelve Apostles of The Church of Jesus Christ of Latter-day Saints.*

Language matters, what we think, what we tell ourselves makes a difference. The messages that our bodies subconsciously send us matter, like me not breathing right and keeping myself in a state of panic. We can take control and heal, change our thoughts and actions, our subliminal messages and our behaviors through our self-talk and the language we use.

Jody Moore explains just how we can do that in her book, *Better Than Happy* and her several podcast episodes. The idea of consciously changing our thoughts to create our desired feelings or outcomes. I have read her book and implemented her strategies, and they worked for me. I have improved the way that I speak to myself and others. I have also been more selective with the messages I watch or listen to and let into my heart and mind.

I love music, it can have an impact on our mood and thoughts. While traveling for training for work, there's a stretch of road through Wyoming where service is limited. The few radio channels that are even available are gospel stations. I have heard a few gems that I have collected over the years. Like many of the conference talks that I read again and again, there are songs that I listen to over and over. On my last trip, I found and added a song to my spiritual playlist. It is called "Make It Through." The lyrics remind me that if I am still, I will be able to hear God's soft voice. If I keep choosing life and breath, then I will be successful. I need that encouragement and reminder to get me through my difficulties.

Another important reminder: "Each new morning is a gift from God. Even the air we breathe is a loving loan from Him.

He preserves us from day to day and supports us from one moment to another. Therefore, our first noble deed of the morning should be a humble prayer of gratitude." ~ *Russell M. Nelson then President of The Church of Jesus Christ of Latter-day Saints.*

I am so grateful for the breath of life, and that I have this amazing opportunity called mortality to expand my capacities.

CHAPTER TWENTY-ONE

Rock Bottom

OUR FAMILY has the typical issues other families have as well as the ones that are unique to us. We are all trying to manage our individual and collective blessings and trials. For the most part, we do very well. I would like to think I contributed to that with my constant reinforcement that we needed to treat family better than anyone else. When I was growing up, we did not always treat each other well. As I got older, I became confused as to why we would treat the most important people in our lives with the least amount of respect. With my own children, I insisted that maintaining their relationships with their siblings was top priority. I know that losing my sister and not having a close relationship with my brother contributed to that. If my kids were not getting along with each other, they were not allowed to have friends over, and if they had friends in our home, they or their friends were not allowed to disrespect their siblings.

I am not naive to the reality that things did not always happen as I would have hoped, but overall, it was more of a success than not; at least my children let me hold onto that belief. As adults, they share stories with me of things that took place unbeknownst to me. They make me wonder where in the heck I was when all of those things were taking place. My kids and I also do not recollect things the same way. If I was in the room, apparently, I was not present. I have tried to justify that I was preoccupied with my troubles, marital stresses, dealing with my mom, trying to resolve past trauma, pushing through physical pain, and making mental lists of all the things that needed to be accomplished. I believe there are reasons why we are better grandparents than parents, because by then, we are usually more settled.

I have become more settled by dealing with some of my difficulties, learning to breathe, and letting go of things. I have been creating more space for calm in my life, learning to trust more, and not fight the process. Other times, my weaknesses or burdens can become so dense that I just sink to the bottom. We deal with heavy things in our family, and at varying times, that weight shifts to different people and problems. For years we dealt with several substantial issues all at once. I have shared my hefty trials and touched on some of my mother's as well. In addition to those and others, we all carry the weight of our son and brother, Skyler. With his permission, I would like to share some of our experiences in dealing with him as he carries his immense inner conflicts.

When Skyler was young, he displayed great intellect. At the age of three, he liked to run the VCR and watch movies. We owned several Disney movies, and each of the kids had their favorites. We discovered that if we laid out all of the black tapes without the cases and asked Skyler to hand us a certain movie, that he could do it. He did not know how to read yet, and they were all identical except for the movie title name and font. He could hand us all twenty plus movies as requested. We assumed by recognizing the different fonts. He was not really talking but would repeat phrases; he struggled through and had to take his time. He liked to run around on his curled toes. A family member and I thought that he was showing signs of autism. Scott did not want to have him tested, but I filled out a questionnaire and found that he and another one of my children had enough points to fall on the spectrum. I figured the questionnaire to be a faulty measurement tool.

Skyler's second-grade teacher suggested he be tested for attention deficit disorder or ADD. He passed that test conducted by the school. We struggled through third grade and decided to throw that year out the window. In fourth grade, his teacher had a son with Asperger's. I was taking classes, and every research paper I turned in was on autism or Asperger's. I was trying to learn and find answers and therapies I could implement at home. At a parent-teacher conference, I asked specifically about my son's behaviors.

She was relieved and replied, "I didn't know how I was going to bring it up, but most days I can't tell who is worse, your son or mine?"

I requested that the school test him again and was told that he would not qualify for special services due to his good grades, high scores, and presidential awards. I was less concerned with the services than the diagnosis. I made an appointment with Primary Children's Hospital but had to wait three months before he could be seen.

In the meantime, the school conducted their testing and found my son to be average. They explained that in the three areas, he needed to have a score of ten in each. Skyler's scores were eights and nines. As a mother, you know when things don't sit right, and that did not sit right with me. I kept the appointment at Primary.

His diagnosis was anxiety, attention deficit—not hyper, and pervasive developmental disorder not otherwise specified, it is on the autism spectrum. Now that my son is older, he rejects part of that diagnosis, it makes him mad. He is adamant that he is NOT autistic, he admits he has the other two. Over the years, we put tools and management practices in place. He was always very high functioning; most people were unaware that he even had anything going on. Where it stood out the most was in his organization and time management skills. In middle school, he was given multiple assignments leading up to a completed science fair project and presentation. Of course, he could not manage all of the individual parts and ended up doing his entire project the night before and winning the fair with his experiment and presentation. However, his grade was a C because he did not hand in all of the individual assignments.

He was athletic and played all the sports in middle school. He stood a foot taller than the other boys. Being the mother that I was, I knew nothing about sports, so I thought all of my kids did great at everything they did. Scott, on the other hand, could see all the traveling violations, double dribbles, and missed plays. It was hard to tell Skyler that he needed to do better when he was the lead scorer and rebounder. He quit growing at six foot four inches tall, and he quit improving. He had natural talent but lacked try. Everything always came so easy to him; he did not have to work hard for anything. He received good grades by doing the bare minimum, he always got by and did not see the need to put forth much effort. He started smoking pot in high school. Scott wanted to kick him out of our home his senior year with all the trouble he was giving us; he was defiant, lying, and doing drugs. I pleaded with Scott to endure it until we made sure he received his diploma. Skyler graduated and, with help, secured a great summer job. He had quite a bit of money for college. Although, while being away from home and his structure, he ended up going into a deep depression, was arrested for drugs, and flunked out of school.

He returned home for a while but couldn't follow the rules for keeping a job and staying off drugs. He slept in his car, and we hoped that was rock bottom for him. It was short-lived as my mother took him in against our advice. She enabled him to sleep all day, stay up playing video games all night, and not work. She put a roof over his head and food in his belly and let him hang out and smoke pot. He was living his best life. His girlfriend moved in with them until my mom decided she finally had enough. Skyler and his girlfriend moved to Vernal, Utah, where they continued their dysfunctional relationship.

Eventually, Skyler called us from jail. He wanted us to come bail him out and bring him home. We both decided to let him sit there and figure things out. He was not there long as he found a friend that helped him get out. That did not last long, though, because Skyler went straight to a party, got drunk, and started acting up. People at the party called the cops, and they took him right back to jail. Scott and I argued about it. We went back and forth with the many possible outcomes. We were stuck between a rock and a hard spot. We drove to Vernal to assess the situation. Neither of us slept well, and finally, about four in the morning, we decided to leave the motel and go retrieve our son.

What we wanted to see happen did not happen. My mother took him back in and made it very easy for him to maintain his addictions. He struggled to keep a job, attend family functions, and manage his hygiene and overall well-being. His girlfriend filed a restraining order against him but later called him to come to her rescue. He went and was arrested once again for violating the order. A year or so later, his ex-girlfriend, that same girl, passed away from a drug overdose. Her family had anticipated it, and we accepted that Skyler might very well have a similar outcome.

My mom would get frustrated and complain, and I would remind her that she chose the situation against our will, and she was the only one who could change it. On and off, for the better part of ten years, he lived with my mom. He did get and keep a job for the last two of those years. He and my mom would argue and fight, and at separate times, they would each try to drag me in the middle of their many disputes. His depression and transition to meth was apparent, even though he thought he had everyone fooled. We did what we could, but it was difficult to help people who refused to help themselves. My mom was part of the problem with her mental health and manipulation. I didn't know who or what to believe. I advised my mom to call the cops and or get a restraining order. Our family discussed getting a restraining order for them as they needed to be separated, but determined it would cause more problems if she would not support it, and let him move right back in.

Finally, on December 30, 2024, I received a phone call at 2:22 in the morning. It was the police, and she had called them. They arrested Skyler, and he stayed the night in jail but was released the very next day. However, my mom was finally ready to put a restraining order in place. After a week or so, with the holidays, it was approved. They were ordered not to be around each other for three years.

Scott, the girls, and I had to go get his things and move them into his truck and a storage trailer on a piece of property we owned. Skyler bounced around at different friends' houses for a week or so and was in constant contact with us for his things and a place to stay. He said it would be temporary as he had quit his job just two weeks prior in anticipation of his online girlfriend coming to get him and move him to Salt Lake with her. After a family meeting, reminding each other to be strong, not give into his pleadings, and not loan him money, Scott and I caved, or at least that was some people's opinion.

Several days after the pep-talk, we were still at a loss as to what to do. We concluded that we had no idea what we were doing, and we needed help from someone who did. Scott and I knelt down to pray and pleaded for guidance and direction.

Skyler had been living ten minutes away for the better part of ten years, and he hardly came around. On occasion, he would show up for a family dinner, a holiday, a wedding, or family pictures. He was usually late and always high. If all of his hopes and wishes came true, he would have moved away with his online girlfriend and who knows how long it would have been before we saw him again. Scott and I decided that we would provide him with the perfect scenario for her to come rescue him. Skyler was the only one surprised when she never showed up. It took a couple of hours of grief and him consulting the tarot cards before he could consider a plan B.

We listed his options and helped with problem solving. The option he liked most was to live in a small camper we had rounded up and park it on our vacant piece of property.

Our family believed, as we had several times in the past, that this had to be his rock bottom. Just getting away from my mom and out of that house started to help. He sold his truck, purchased the camper, and paid off an outstanding loan. He had enough money left over to pay for several weeks of living expenses while he figured things out. He got his old job back and stopped smoking pot. He said he had gone off meth cold a while ago. He started going to the gym and lifting weights again. He was looking better and even put on some needed weight. After a month or so, we discovered that he had been lying about working and the pot. He was almost out of money but was able to pick up a construction job for a few days. He purchased a thousand-dollar truck to help him get back and forth. However, he could no longer afford to keep gas in it and was already back to needing rides and money.

Only recently did I learn that my mother started giving him her pain pills and medication when he was in middle school. He had been playing football and got hurt. He didn't need them, but she offered her pills to him, and I'm sure he didn't know any better. It started a habit of him asking my mom or her offering a painkiller with every bump, scrape, and bruise he received. He said he does not blame her, but I am undecided. He had many other challenges and shared that the pills were not enough to quiet the voices in his mind. He transitioned to marijuana and embraced the natural health benefits and treatment it offered. We learned that in his senior year, after previously refusing treatment for his ADD, he requested and started filling a prescription for it. Later, he transitioned to meth and who knows what else. He shared that the entire time he lived with Grandma, she was very generous with her narcotics.

He had lived in the little camper for three months when one Monday night, he called me, inebriated and crying. He decided to have a pity party and spend his last ten borrowed dollars on a fifth of tequila. Alcohol is not his drug of choice, and it does not look good on him. Through tears, he told me that he wanted to die. He has struggled with suicidal tendencies in the past but had convinced himself that he was doing better. I went and picked him up in a blizzard and took him to get a blessing. After weighing all of my options, it was the best thing I could do. It was an amazing blessing, and once I got him back to my house and in the shower, I wrote it down as I assumed he would not remember it in the morning. I snuggled my twenty-eight-year-old son until he fell asleep. The next day, he apologized and was embarrassed by his behavior. He was surprised that he called his "mommy" but was grateful that I came to his aid.

The first time he called me struggling with thoughts of suicide he was scared; it was years ago in his early twenties. He was having a panic attack and overwhelmed with thoughts to harm himself; he didn't want to listen to them, but he didn't know what to do. I had an inkling that he was struggling and had already checked into the best course of action. I took him down to the University of Utah Hospital emergency room, and they took it from there. I stayed with him as he described to them his preferred method of suicide; although, it was hard to hear. I learned a lot about how he processed stress and challenges. While waiting, it felt like it took forever, but in reality, it was only a couple of hours before they could secure all of the necessary approvals from the insurance.

They admitted him to their mental health facility. He was there for a week or so, then transitioned to weekly outpatient therapy. I would drive him to Layton for his appointments and figured if I was already there, I might as well make appointments for myself. After a few months, his therapy was finished, and I had too many things going on to continue making that two hour trip each way, every week. I started seeing someone locally; she would drive over from Evanston to see her patients in the valley. I was seeking help to manage the challenges with my son. Without seeing him, she predicted that he probably had other undiagnosed conditions, but at that point, it would have been difficult to untangle what was Skyler and what was the drugs.

The second time Skyler threatened suicide was very different. He kept saying, "Mom, you should be worried about me."

I told him, "Son, I always worry about you."

I listed all of his available options, but he didn't want to take advantage of any of them. I realized that he was trying to manipulate me. It can be tricky because you never know for sure and you don't want to be wrong in a life-and-death situation. I did not feel this was the case at that time. I cautioned him that if that is what he was determined to do, I would probably not be able to stop him, as I could not be with him all the time. I bore my testimony that God is in charge of life and death, and if he were to be successful, it was because it was his time. If it was not his time, he would not be able to complete it.

He never threatened suicide again after our conversation. When he called me crying, it was different from the other times. It was more that he was sad and wished for death, not that he was going to cause harm to himself. I tried to remember that he was working with a greater degree of difficulty. I do my best, but it is like walking a tightrope with him on my shoulders while trying to balance my family on one hand and everything else on the other.

Some of the best advice I have received is, "You cannot save your children, only the Savior can save them." That truth has relieved a lot of pressure for me, but I still feel the weight bearing down as I try to stay steady. Until he decides that he has hit rock bottom, this will be an ongoing issue; one that needs to be handled with constant instruction from above as we continue to navigate and do damage control in moments of crisis. I don't know what I'm doing. I just try to stay close enough to the Spirit so He can whisper in my ear and tell me what to do or remind me that we will make it through.

The significance of hitting rock bottom is that you can find Jesus there, He is literally our rock and our Redeemer. If Skyler will decide to grab onto that rock and hold on, he will discover that Jesus is the only thing that can truly lift him.

"And now, my sons, remember, remember that it is upon the rock of our Redeemer, who is Christ, the Son of God, that ye must build your foundation; that when the devil shall send forth his mighty winds, yea, his shafts in the whirlwind, yea, when all his hail and his mighty storm shall beat upon you, it shall have no power over you to drag you down to the gulf of misery and endless wo, because of the rock upon which ye are built, which is a sure foundation, a foundation whereon if men build they cannot fall." ~ *The Book of Mormon Helaman 5:12.*

Con·tent

In a state of peaceful
happiness.

CHAPTER TWENTY-TWO

Do The Work

*I*T's 2025, and as I write this, Scott's and my disagree-ments are now few and far between, resolved quicker and more productive than they were in the past. Most of them have always revolved around our son, and that is still the case. We are in a committed marriage, and we are work-ing toward becoming more unified. Prayer has been added as part of our important decision-making. We kneel in prayer to resolve misunderstandings, get clarity, counsel, and direction. We know that what we do affects each other, our family, and close friends. With the decline of marriage in our country, we hope to maintain ours and be a good example to those around us. Marriage is one of the hardest things you can do; it is also one of the most important. There are many opportunities each and every day to throw the white flag. Marriage requires you to continue to set your pride and selfish or unrealistic desires aside for the greater good. Again and again, we choose each other every single day.

That being said, I do not believe that you should stay in an abusive or unhealthy relationship for the sake of staying mar-ried. No one is capable of keeping a family afloat by themselves.

If you have a partner determined to sink the boat, get on the life raft and save yourself and your children. Better yet, if you can manage it, give your partner the raft and you keep the boat. However, I have witnessed many people surrendering because they are unwilling to put forth the required effort. I have also had discussions with friends that unreasonably believe if they left the difficulties they were facing, that they could go find someone else with no problems. I have been married three times and have lots of friends and family examples, and I can tell you with certainty that there is not one human that has NO issues. *Everyone has issues.* Everyone has something that you would have to "put up with." I personally believe that the real problems lie in how people are unable to face their issues and their unwillingness or inability to acknowledge and work on improving them.

Our circumstances matter; how we have developed matters. It affects our tolerance and abilities to "put up with" or fix certain things better than others. Scott and I have had many discussions when things happen with the couples around us, and we ask ourselves, how would we have handled that? What do you think could have been done to stay away from that situation altogether? What can we do differently and how do we avoid a similar demise? Do they have enough to rebuild? Would we?

Some of our answers include be willing to do the work, apologize and forgive, let go of things that are not serving you in a positive manner, and don't turn little things into big things, like I used to do. And we apply Lance's advice, "If in one year from the issue it will not matter, it is not worth your time."

But whatever you do, don't let go of your correct beliefs and convictions. Do not lose yourself and shrink, even if you don't see eye to eye, for the sake of not making waves. Make waves when absolutely necessary. I love the quote, "A smooth sea never made a skilled sailor." ~ *Franklin D. Roosevelt.*

A voyage with no waves is probably not worth taking; you might as well stay on the shore. I am not saying that you ignore a weather warning and set sail in the middle of a hurricane to see if you can survive it. Yet you must develop your skills to be able to handle a storm when it comes; *and they will come.* Partners need to be increasing in ability and capacity to do so, personally and as a couple. Eventually, the devil will send forth his whirlwinds and mighty storms that will beat upon you, and there is a good chance you will get hit repeatedly. In order to get to your destination, you have to cross the water—you can't go over it, around it, or under it. You must go through it.

When children, parents, family, and friends cross over, or physical, mental, emotional, and financial trials come, will they bring you together or tear you apart? Will you get through the storms together?

When our friend, Lance, passed away, Scott and I grew closer. We learned from it and shored up some things. We concluded that eventually everyone we know and love is going to die.

If you are already not doing well, trials will exacerbate your issues. If you are managing or thriving, chances are you will continue to do so without it thrashing you to pieces. On occasion, severe storms can get into pinholes and cracks you never knew existed. If this happens and your boat gets destroyed, do you have the skills, the desire to clean up the mess and rebuild your marriage? Do you have the reserves to replace what was lost? This is when many people walk away from the wreckage, if they make it that far. Only you can answer these questions for yourself. No one can do it for you, and one partner cannot sustain it alone. Work together or let them find someone who will labor with them if you refuse. If you are willing and able, pick up a hammer and get to work. There are times that I have had to sit and watch my husband accomplish many tasks by himself as I was unable to assist either mentally, physically, or both. I am not referring to those times—when you want to but you can't. I am talking about when you withhold your assistance.

A marriage is best when functioning by the same rules as Grace. You love each other where you are but don't intend for you, your relationship, or your partner to stay that way. Yet, you must still wait, timing is everything. Learn and grow, repent and forgive, do better, be better for yourselves and your spouse, show compassion and mercy for weaknesses, and lean on and sustain each other. Share the yoke and the burden together and with Jesus. "For [his] yoke is easy, and [his] burden is light." ~ *Holy Bible Mathew 11:30.*

Some fall into complacency and turn a blind eye. That is not improvement, that is denial and avoidance. Some partners refuse to accept any blame and want the other half to make all of the adjustments—that is not right—if you get there together, you must fix it together. My marriage has improved with every year that passes, not by accident but by doing the work required for the sake of our family and out of love and respect for each other.

Do not misunderstand, we are not perfect, nor do we have everything all figured out. We've made our share of mistakes, but we have both made changes, compromises, and improvements. We have learned a few things through trial and error and by having great examples around us modeling what to do and other examples teaching us what not to do.

I started really struggling driving myself to the temple every month before COVID hit. My anxiety was increasing, and I had to push myself to keep going. I didn't tell anyone then but having the temple closed down helped me for a short time. However, taking away the option made me realize how much I needed it. I shared these thoughts and feelings with my husband. He offered to drive me to the temple. Although I could not go in, I just wanted to get as close as possible—so I could feel it. He has been driving me almost every month for the last four-ish years; very seldom do I go alone. We plan a monthly temple date together. I go to the temple, and he goes to a little pub a block away. Afterward, we have lunch and get groceries and other required shopping. He loves me and knows how important it is for me to regularly attend the temple, so he makes sure I can get there. We work together to help each other keep our individual and collective goals. I told Scott years ago, "I wish you were attending the temple with me, but whether you choose to go or not, I want the blessings for myself."

In one of my online religion classes through BYUI, a topic discussed was that of work. Until then, I had never thought about work being a gospel principle. I am not talking about everyone getting a paying job, although that is part of it. I am referring to how the Lord loves effort. If you search for the subject "work" on the official church website, churchofjesuschrist. org, you will find lots of resources.

From the LDS church website, we are told that:

- There is No Substitute for Work.

- Building a strong family takes hard work, and part of that work is teaching our children how to work.

- Though some may see work as something to avoid, the gospel teaches that working for and with our families brings great blessings.

- Work is always a spiritual necessity even if, for some, work is not an economic necessity.

"...how often the scriptures have admonished us to cease to be idle and to be productive in all of our labors. ...Teaching children the joy of honest labor is one of the greatest of all gifts you can bestow upon them." ~ *Elder Tom Perry, former apostle of The Church of Jesus Christ of Latter-day Saints.*

The best place to teach and learn how to work is in the family unit. When the kids were teenagers, they liked to take advantage of the fact that I wanted to keep the sabbath and their dad did not believe it was necessary. They would threaten to ask him to buy them pizza on Sunday even though he never did. They tried to manipulate the system as most teenagers do. One Sunday, we were arriving home from church, and Scott was out cutting and stacking firewood. Almost in unison the kids begged me, "Tell Dad we do not work on Sundays."

I took advantage of the teaching opportunity, and after getting in the house, I went straight to change out of my dress and into work clothes. I went out and helped Scott with the firewood. Scott and I may not have seen eye to eye on all things gospel related, but we were always in agreement with the principle to labor together temporally and teach our kids the value of a strong work ethic.

President Hinckley pleaded that we, "Work at our responsibility as parents as if everything in life counted on it, because in fact everything in life does count on it." ~ *Elder Dallin H. Oaks of the Quorum of the Twelve Apostles of The Church of Latter-day Saints.*

I am grateful for my husband and his work ethic. We have both taught this to our children. Scott showed them how to fish, hunt, process meat, obtain and keep a job, yard work, athletics, firewood, and much more. Our kids witnessed our examples of laboring together, me helping my husband on several occasions, and Scott assisting me with the many household chores. They observed me working hard to increase my education. I taught them to clean, cook, and manage finances. I have taken several classes or seminars on the subject and excitedly share what I learn. When my kids were older, they asked why we pay 10 percent of our earnings to the church, as logically it seems reasonable to spend that money elsewhere.

I started to answer, but stopped, turned to Scott, and asked, "Scott, why do we pay our tithing?"

He replied, "Because it makes our 90 percent go further."

It is true, and with my several money classes and books, even non-member, reputable, financial experts will advise that giving charitable donations is wise and positively affects the ebb and flow of our money. I agree with the philosophy of working smarter, not harder, and paying tithing is the smartest way to make our money work for us.

In the gospel of Jesus Christ, we call our labors, missionary work, family history work, temple work. We are encouraged to be engaged in good works and so on. Everything we do in life and living the gospel takes hard work and effort. Sometimes in my marriage, my job, with my health, or living the gospel, I have not always had the capacity to seemingly work as hard as others. What God can see that humans cannot, is that like The Widow's Mite, I give all that I have. ~ *Holy Bible Mark 12:42-44.*

I love that God knows me perfectly and that He sees the time and effort I put in. At times, I have given more in my abundance, and at other times, when I was poor in spirit or was experiencing physical or mental poverty, I gave less, but it is what I had to give and He accepted my offerings.

"... The Lord will accept that which is enough, with a good deal more pleasure and satisfaction than that which is too much and unnecessary." ~ *Joseph F. Smith, in Conference Report, Oct. 1912, 133–34.*

Although that quote is taken out of context, I have learned that it is true and can be applied to the time and effort we put forth on behalf of our families, our marriages, and our work in the gospel. All of our efforts will one day be generously rewarded; it will all be worth it.

CHAPTER TWENTY-THREE

Worth It

*T*HE MOST IDEAL MARRIAGE I have had the privilege of witnessing was my Grandma and Grandpa Walker's. I can still see their white house by the canal. The pasture outback with corrals, a large hay barn, and the tack shed. My siblings, cousins, neighborhood kids and I would play in the yard and haystack building forts and tunnels. I would get all itchy, but it didn't stop me from doing it. We used to sneak into the tack shed and eat handfuls of horse grain. It would take forever to chew the dry sweet oats and seeds. My husband pointed out years later how unsanitary that was. Of course, I was oblivious at the time. The tack shed was not far from the back porch entry to the house that held the coats, boots, a bench, the washer, dryer, and a chest freezer. The porch led into the kitchen. It had white painted cabinets, appliances, table and chairs, a heater, and an old cooking stove. It was an older home with inefficient heat. I would warm myself by that heater and take note of Grandma's cooking.

The house smelled like a combination of bacon, syrup, oil paints, and Zest soap—some of the best scents. There was a cupboard in the short hall that, when opened, had a cut out you could shimmy through to get into the bathroom. We used it as a secret passageway when playing. The back bedroom had almost a sitting area with a closet before stepping down to get to the dresser and the bed. We had many imaginary adventures in that room.

Back in the hall across from the bathroom was a door that opened to the food pantry and a steep set of stairs leading up to what used to be my uncle's room, then later my grandma's paint studio, and it was my room when I lived with them briefly while my parents were going through their divorce. On the other side of the house was an open living and dining area, a large master closet that doubled as a hideout before stepping down into Grandma and Grandpa's room—we never played in there.

One winter, the Clinton Walker family loaded into an old school bus my grandpa had purchased, and he drove us to his brother's property in Robertson, Wyoming, to go tubing down the hills, play in the snow, and drink hot chocolate. There was at least one snowmobile I can remember that would pull the tubes back up the hill; we enjoyed that fun activity most of the day. That family outing happened once, but annually, Grandpa and his twenty siblings faithfully took turns holding family reunions. They continue to this day; although, not with the same respect and reverence for the importance of family that I felt as a kid. My siblings and I loved getting together and playing with all the cousins. We dug in the dirt and hid under large tree branches, we were resourceful, building stick forts and hideouts and had a blast. I miss that part of my childhood, that special family connection.

I have more frequent memories of making macramé beaded necklaces, playing the Mork and Mindy card game with the Styrofoam eggs containing teeth and claw marks, and eating many meals at Grandma and Grandpa's table. We had family get-togethers, Christmas parties, and my sweet sixteen in that farmhouse. My grandma gave me oil painting lessons and would sketch me paper dolls with fashionable wardrobes. Grandma was an amazing artist, and most of the family still hang her treasured paintings. I enjoyed drawing, sketching, and painting. At one time because of my grandma's artistic and my mom's sewing abilities, I aspired to be a fashion designer. It was short-lived; I did not inherit either of their full talents.

Grandma tried to make everyone feel special—she catered to everyone's needs and waited on Grandpa. When I was a teenager, my grandpa was literally two feet from the fridge. He could have turned and grabbed the handle, but no, he called to Grandma, "Merlin, will you come get me a glass of milk?" And she did. I was dumbfounded *at the time* that he couldn't get his own milk. I thought he was taking advantage of her kind nature.

Years later, I can't remember how long Scott and I had been married, but he called for me to grab him a beer, and I stopped what I was doing and waited on him. I recalled the experience with my grandparents and finally understood, *you serve those you love.*

After my sister passed, my grandparents went on an LDS mission to Nauvoo. They were tour guides, and my grandma got to teach paint classes and work in the bakery. My grandpa was a blacksmith and made horseshoe souvenirs and other items. I missed them when they were gone, and the respite I got from them and their home. After their mission, things were different. They were busy dealing with other family issues and priorities that demanded their time and attention, and for a couple of years, they moved out to a ranch called the Ponderosa.

I remember spending some time out there in the summer, playing in that old farmhouse and staying the night in the guest bedroom. It had an antique bedroom set that my grandma had refinished. My cousins and I would explore the pastures, creeks, and corrals while looking for treasures. One time, I was allowed to take a friend out with me. On a separate occasion when I was there, I remember getting upset and freaking out in front of everyone, although I can't remember why.

With Grandma and Grandpa's attention elsewhere and along with my parents' divorce, I felt like I was being phased out of the family. Contact became limited, my brief, tense stay with them during the divorce ended with hard feelings on my end, mostly with my dad.

They showed up for my high school graduation and wedding reception, but I never heard from them or any of my dad's family while I was serving in the military. Our relationship was almost non-existent. When I got back from the military, Grandma and Grandpa no longer lived in the white farmhouse on the hill. They had moved down to their property adjacent to where we were living when my sister passed away.

I wanted them back in my life.

I started going to visit them with Saxen when she was a baby. Grandma helped me with all of my kids from the time they were infants. She would occasionally watch her great-grandchildren. The kids and I, and sometimes Scott, spent more time with them over the years. They attended our kids' baby blessings, birthday parties, baptisms, Young Women events, Eagle Scout activities, some sporting events, and graduations. They showed up and supported my family.

However, it was conditional as we were still tiptoeing around my dad's wife's rules. Grandma wanted to try and fix everything and make everyone happy. I think it broke her heart having contention in the family. My grandpa wanted me to apologize and thought that would solve everything. I knew it would not. Meanwhile, I don't think we ever left their house without an ice cream cone or one of Grandma's famous slushies and hugs. Grandpa would usually make his memorable hee-haw bray, and ask, "How do you like them apples?" or he would grab your calf while barking just like a dog. If you were there in the evening, they were watching *Wheel of Fortune, Jeopardy, Bob Hope, MASH, Red Skeleton,* or *Hee-Haw,* all popular television shows of their time.

After Scott and I got married and moved to our property, we were in the same ward as my grandparents. When I became active again, I got to see them almost weekly from across the chapel. If I didn't see them, I still knew when they were there. They would hang their coats on the same hangers, and my grandpa's beige felt cowboy hat would be carefully placed on the rack above them. They were not labeled, but I'm pretty sure everyone knew that was Clinton and Merlin's spot. While still living at home, they traveled weekly for two years serving a temple mission. As they aged and lost their hearing, you could recognize their presence during sacrament. Loudly, Grandpa would ask, "What did they say?" and then Grandma would repeat everything back to him. It was the sweetest thing. I miss them being at church, their examples, endurance, and testimonies.

My grandpa started suffering from Alzheimer's and dementia. Knowing each other so well after decades of time together, I think Grandma had a system developed to cover for him and finish his thoughts and sentences. I know this helped to offer the appearance that things were not as bad as they really were. Grandpa would be out driving around then get confused and not know where he was or how he had gotten there. When he parked his vehicle, he could not remember where he had parked it. Ultimately, they had to get rid of his pickup. I helped out here and there to give my dad and aunt, their two local children, a small break, as they were required to increase their assistance. I would take my turn getting Grandma and Grandpa out of the house. We would check their mail, and usually, Grandpa would insist on driving around to look for his truck. He was convinced that someone had stolen it. I knew exactly where it was, it had been sold, but he forgot those conversations, so it was easier to drive around and keep searching.

They were able to live in their home much longer than they probably should have, but that is a tortuous decision for a family to make. It was finally taken out of everyone's hands when my grandma ended up falling in the middle of the night as a result of a severe bladder infection. I was available to take her to the doctor and sit with her for a couple of days. The doctor broke the news that they could no longer stay in their home. The children had all of the arrangements made prior, ready to go for when they needed to be implemented. They were moved down to a memory care facility in Taylorsville, Utah, close to their oldest daughter.

I visited them several times even after my grandpa could no longer recognize anyone; even Grandma. I could see the longing in her eyes as she would gaze at him in hopes that he would recall a spec of the love they shared, but he never regained his memory of her. Separating them became necessary as Grandpa's condition worsened. The family and the center would take Grandma to go visit him until he passed away in May of 2019. They were married for seventy-two years; that is amazing to me. Some people don't live that long, let alone get to spend that entire time with their high school sweetheart.

The love and respect my grandparents developed was impressive, and even though I didn't know how to label it when I was young, I still felt and recognized it. It also took me years to put my finger on what I experienced in their home; it was the Spirit. On their wall hung a medium framed cross-stitch of the Savior's face with His quote, "I never said it would be easy, I only said it would be worth it."

They made marriage look pretty easy and created a very high standard for others to live up to; although, I am sure they had their secret difficulties. After almost twenty-eight years for Scott and me, we are now hopeful that one day we might get close to what they created, that all of our work and effort on behalf of our marriage, although it has not been easy for us, will be worth it as well.

My grandma passed away right after Christmas in 2021. Her two daughters were by her side, and one reported that Grandpa stepped forward from a group of warm, glowing spirits who were there to retrieve her. My aunt marveled in the love she could feel from the other side. It was unlike anything she had ever felt. I know that we are going to be so happy when we finally get to have our own reunion with all of our loved ones waiting for us in the spirit world. I am grateful that my grandparents lived a long and happy life, and that I was able to spend many years with them.

CHAPTER TWENTY-FOUR

Forty Years

SEPTEMBER 2025 will be the fortieth anniversary of my sister's passing. Some days feel like I have not seen her in forever. Other days, it is like it was yesterday, and we were just riding motorcycles, arguing, or playing in our room. I can be pulled back in time to relive moments, see glimpses of what was, or perfectly recall receiving the news on that wounded couch. Now I see her angelic silhouette throughout my life, watching over me and my family, protecting us, guiding us. I know our loved ones are on the other side. I believe the spirit world is not a location far away, another planet, or in a different realm. They are just on the other side, here next to us, but out of our mortal sight; and if we could see them, they would be within our reach. This is my opinion and experience. I still tell my grandchildren that heaven is above us in the sky. I'm not sure they're ready for my full explanation.

The children of Israel wandered in the desert for forty years, Noah and his family endured rain for forty days and forty nights, Jesus fasted for forty days; I believe there is biblical significance to the number forty. To me, it represents a transition, the end of one thing and the start of something new, a completion.

Once in the promised land, the Israelites had to work for their food. Manna was no longer distributed, but God trusted that they could now provide for themselves and showed them how. Noah, his family, and all the animals had to start over and rebuild a community and repopulate the earth, but God orchestrated a way for it to be accomplished. Immediately after fasting, Satan came to tempt Jesus. After rejecting all of his absurd proposals, was when angels came and ministered to Him and strengthened Him.

When I was taking the institute class, there was a woman new to our area in attendance. She had studied the significance of numbers in the scriptures, and I remember her sharing that the number forty may not have been the exact increment of time, rather forty represented a period of time that was equal to, "as long as it takes."

Maybe the Israelites wandered in the wilderness for as long as it took them to learn what God needed them to learn before being ready to live in the promised land. Maybe it flooded for as long as it took to cover the earth and clean it so Noah, his family, and the animals could reinhabit the earth. And maybe Jesus fasted for as long as it took to become vulnerable enough for Satan to think he could overcome him.

God knows for sure; I am just speculating. Time increments aside, I know that after those experiences came the blessings; arrival to the promised land, a rainbow with a promise, and the ministering of angels. However, their work was not over, it changed, it increased. Regardless of it being exactly forty years or days and nights or for as long as it takes. I am approaching the forty-year mark of Terri's passing and I feel a significant work just ahead. ~ *Bible stories summary.*

I am looking forward to the next chapters of my life. My

arrival, my rainbow; my association with angels. I used to listen to a vinyl record after my sister passed away. It included dialogue between a mother and her son after she gets sick. Right before she dies, she tries explaining that she needs to leave him. He was confused as to how he would know that she was okay and how he would still feel her if she were gone. She testified that families can be together forever, and she would send signs of her continued existence and love. One sign is revealed in the title of the song, "I'll Build You a Rainbow."

Every time I see a rainbow, I think of my sister and remember that God has provided a way through the temple sealing ordinance for families to be together for time and all eternity, and that I will get to be with my sister again. That song helped me at the time, it was the only explanation I received about how death worked, because we didn't talk about it much. I did believe there was a home in heaven where she went to live without me.

I understand death much differently now. It is one of the strongest convictions I possess. I believe when it is your time, nothing can stop it. Regardless of how you die, including suicide, it would not happen if it was not your time. People do not show up in heaven and God says, I was not expecting you today. I do not believe that we can worry someone dead or hope and pray them alive. God knows everything, and He is in control. I do believe that we can affect our quality of life through the choices we make, and our thoughts can determine our actions, but our ultimate time of passing is in the hands of God. I do not believe in accidents either, only perfectly orchestrated events that reveal divine intervention. I have had too many experiences, heard and read too many stories to think otherwise.

Another scriptural example of forty days and nights is when Moses went up to Mount Sinai to receive personalized instructions from the Lord. I too, have been receiving instruction from God, lessons that have been crafted just for me. My trials have taught me many things, as well as reading and studying the scriptures, obedience to the commandments, and making and keeping covenants. I go often to the mount to receive further light and knowledge that can only be found in the temple. When I come back from the mount and find my family, friends, and associates not living in accordance with what I believe, I love them. I try to stay strong and be a good example. I hold fast to the promises that I have made and cling to the promises the Lord has made to me if I remain faithful.

I know that everyone gets their forty, or as long as it takes for them to get to where Heavenly Father needs them to be. In the early years of our marriage, I used to tell Scott, "I will not wait twenty years for you to marry me in the temple."

I wanted it then.

After eighteen years of marriage, I told him, "I will wait as long as it takes because you are worth the wait."

It took me that long to let myself fully accept his love without feeling like he was going to find any reason to stop loving me and leave. By then, I had also learned that I could not force spiritual growth, I could only try to cultivate it. "If you want something to last forever, you treat it differently." ~ *Elder F Burton Howard.*

I want to be with Scott and my family forever, and until that happens, I will keep wandering with them, learning from them, loving them, protecting our relationships, and attending the temple often. Because the truth is, just because I am an active member of the church does not mean that I have arrived where I need to be either. Although I am trying to live the gospel to the best of my ability, I am still wandering. I am just willing to go where God leads me. I am grateful that I have such an amazing husband and family to wander with me.

At times, the path I needed to take had been made clear. Other times, I felt that I just had to keep inching my way in what I hoped was the right direction until the course was revealed. I know where I have been, and I know where I eventually want to end up. I am excited to see what steps God will have me take moving forward. The unknown is scary for me; I hate surprises. As many times as I try to visualize, worry, or predict what might be over the edge, it never turns out the way I thought. Things might be hard, but I know that they turn out better because God's plan for me will always be more than I could ever imagine for myself. And even though I am eagerly awaiting my reunion with my sister and all of my loved ones on the other side, I can and will wait. I know that I still have work to do, and that they are watching and assisting me with my work. I am better able to feel them cheering me on, and I am working on tapping into their assistance.

I love my life, and I am grateful for all of the good, the bad, and the ugly. I know that everything I have been through has helped me to learn and grow, develop hope, faith and charity.

"Above all the attributes of godliness and perfection, charity is the one most devoutly to be desired. Charity is more than love, far more; it is everlasting love, perfect love, the pure love of Christ which endureth forever. It is love so centered in righteousness that the possessor has no aim or desire except for the eternal welfare of his own soul and for the souls of those around him." ~ *Mormon Doctrine by former Elder Bruce R. McConkie of The Church of Jesus Christ of Latter-day Saints. 2 Nephi. 26:30; Moroni. 7:47; 8:25–26 from The Book of Mormon.*

My charitable desires revolve around others' eternal welfare, and my own. I try to give people in my life the time they need to wander; God does. I stopped, mostly, trying to implement my timeline with others. I learned the hard way; it doesn't work anyway. I focus on what I have control over, *me.* I constantly pray to know what I can do to be a help and not a hindrance. I ask what I should stop doing and what I can start doing. I am willing to follow where the Lord takes me. He will never let me get very far in the wrong direction if I am actively seeking His counsel. I give grace and have gotten where I can feel His love and try to help others feel His love for them.

I know that my experiences have all been turned for my good. We are promised in Doctrine and Covenants 90:24: "Search diligently, pray always, and be believing, and all things shall work together for your good, if ye walk uprightly."

I have not always walked uprightly, but I have straightened all of those things out. I know that I have made things right between God and me, with my Savior as my advocate, pleading my case before Him, They both know my degree of difficulty. At times, I think that I would like to undo many things, but then I am reminded that Jesus undoes them, and I would not be me without them. I have learned to like me; I even love myself now. I have come to understand that my experiences are not something to be set aside, or ashamed of, rather things that I get to carry with me, without them weighing me down. They help me interact with more grace and meaning, more understanding, charity, and love. I know that I have a long way to go, but I also have a lot to work with. I have tools and resources at my disposal. I have family, friends, and loved ones on both sides of the veil. If I don't know what the answers are, I always know where to find them, and I know that God will give me all the time that I need to get things figured out.

I wished I would have grasped two concepts better years ago. One is that God looks at sin and weakness differently. "We might define weakness as the limitation on our wisdom, power, and holiness that comes with being human. As mortals we are born helpless and dependent, with various physical flaws and predispositions. We are raised and surrounded by other weak mortals, and their teachings, examples, and treatment of us are faulty and sometimes damaging. In our weak, mortal state we suffer physical and emotional illness, hunger, and fatigue. We experience human emotions like anger, grief, and fear. We lack wisdom, skill, stamina, and strength. And we are subject to temptations of many kinds." ~ *Article on the church website by Wendy Ulrich- "It Isn't a Sin to Be Weak."*

I am absolutely limited in my human wisdom, have flaws, and was raised by other weak mortals that definitely did some damage. To be fair, I have caused damage myself; my husband and children can tell you. I suffer physical and mental illness and fatigue and experience a wide range of human emotions and temptations. I have dealt with many weaknesses that I mistakenly thought were sins. In my misunderstanding about weaknesses, I actually ended up sinning and believing that I was too damaged to be loved, fixed, or forgiven.

"We cannot simply repent of being weak—nor does weakness itself make us unclean. We cannot grow spiritually unless we reject sin, but we also do not grow spiritually unless we accept our state of human weakness, respond to it with humility and faith, and learn through our weakness to trust in God." ~ *Article on the church website by Wendy Ulrich – "It Isn't a Sin to Be Weak."*

The second concept that I did not fully understand was that repentance is not a punishment. I was encouraged to read

The Miracle of Forgiveness. Although the principles are true, I believe that book lacks the love and mercy that God intended to be included in the repentance process.

When I repented the first time for my major sins, I felt it was too easy; I was not punished enough. I continued to sub-consciously punish myself, naively trying to make up for my mistakes. I did not understand that not only is it impossible for me to make up the difference, but that is exactly why we have the Savior, that is His job, not mine.

The idea of daily repentance was foreign to me, and I have not always been great at consistency. At some point I questioned, will I ever reach a day that I need not repent?

The answer is no. Repentance is literally to correct our course, to keep turning to God again and again. I know for me that I cannot create the smallest space between me and God because that is where Satan pushes in. He talks me out of praying, says if I did that one thing then why not one more, I could take care of that later; I am too broken or damaged so why bother, and so on. Through daily repentance or what I like to call, eliminating the gap, every day I can turn back to God. I do not feel that I need to hide from Him, also how do we hide from God when He can see and knows everything. Rather, I am no longer uncomfortable in His presence because I have gotten to know Him. I now lean into Him, draw close to Him even in my sins, my weaknesses, my brokenness, so He can heal, forgive, and lift me. I am no angel, but living the gospel and daily repentance has given me wings.

Harry Emerson Fosdick once wrote: "Some Christians carry their religion on their backs. It is a packet of beliefs and practices which they must bear. At times it grows heavy and they would willingly lay it down, but that would mean a break with old traditions, so they shoulder it again. But real Christians do not carry their religion, their religion carries them. It is not weight; it is wings. It lifts them up, it sees them over hard places, it makes the universe seem friendly, life purposeful, hope real, sacrifice worthwhile. It sets them free from fear, futility, discouragement, and sin—the great enslavers of men's souls. You can know a real Christian, when you see [them], by [their] buoyancy." ~ *Elder L. Tom Perry of the Quorum of the Twelve Apostles of The Church of Jesus Christ of Latter-day Saints.*

CHAPTER TWENTY-FIVE

Choose Joy

ONE OF MY GIRLS wanted to be individually featured in my book. But I could fill chapters with the many challenges they have faced. The hard lessons they have learned and taught me. The tears I have cried for and because of them, their anguish, disappointments, victories, and triumphs. I know that God is aware of their varying degrees of difficulty. I can also fill chapters with stories about how amazing and wonderful they are. How thoughtful they can be and how much they serve me, their dad, their families, friends, and others around them. What great mothers, aunts, wives, partners, and humans they are turning out to be. I love their husbands, significant others, and their children—my grandchildren. I love spending time with them all, individually and collectively.

We spend a lot of time together as a family. Weekly text, phone calls, visits. Usually, a regular gathering or wholesome recreational activity like watching sports, UFC, playing games, golfing, Grizzly hockey, camping, fishing, building or fixing things, and lots of holiday dress-up parties. I could go on and on. We love to be around our family and our friends; it saddens me that my son chooses not to participate as often as

I would like him to, and his choices have dictated his involvement or lack thereof.

Sunday dinner is a standing invitation, with a few exceptions when we are out of town. We take turns cooking, and everyone pitches in and helps out. One of my favorite activities is when we all gather in the kitchen. The grandkids start out helping but end up running around happily playing while the adults keep preparing the meals. Some are cutting, stirring, arranging, but most everyone is there, working together.

Our family is not perfect. We have issues and hard things, but we get along fairly well, and we try to work through the problems we do have. Everyone takes a turn bugging others or being bugged. I try to mediate and be a buffer. I want everyone to love each other and get along, just like my grandma did. My children now understand that we have a good family; growing up I'm not so sure they realized it. They have increased their appreciation for their upbringing, riding horses, motorcycles, camping, fishing, hunting, sleepovers, baking, crafting, sewing, dancing, singing, getting firewood, picking up rocks, chores, dishes, Cleaning Olympics, laundry, playing a variety of sports, and much more. They survived it, and they each have their own stories to tell. It is always amazing to me how many individuals can be present for the same experience and yet we each remember it so differently.

When my kids were young, we had two sets of spiderman boxing gloves. We would let the kids "play box" with them. Saxen and Spring fought fairly, the twins were very competitive and would punch more than they would block. The rest of us would enthusiastically shout advice and remind them all to keep their gloves up. My son and I were opponents one time with specific rules to not hit in the face. I was not expecting it, per the rule, however, Skyler clocked me right in the nose. I removed my gloves and forfeited the bout. I plopped on the couch with my eyes watering, the rest of the family tried unsuccessfully not to laugh.

It was all in good fun, but we each have a different version of that same story. However, I hope the kids all learned the same lesson from those experiences and others. That life is tough; it can punch you in the face and knock you around the ring. I hope we taught them that one can never have too many people in their corner. People that love, support, and encourage them to get back out there and keep fighting, keep moving, and blocking punches. People cheering them on and yelling at them to get back up when life knocks them down. I am so grateful for all the people that are in my corner.

I am told in my patriarchal blessing that my children will "grow" to be valent in the gospel. I often wonder how much fertilizer it will take. I have learned that you cannot prevent bad things from happening to your children, they need to have their own experiences and grooming for who God needs them to be. We can wander with them as they navigate their way through, we can cultivate the ground, lead by example, and hope they follow. Sometimes our kids let Scott and me help or ask for our advice. Other times, we stand in the corner shouting out encouragement or tips and tricks. Sometimes, we have to watch with our mouths shut and let things play out, while we shake our heads. Occasionally, we hold our breath while we wait for them to get back up after they have been knocked down.

Like the children of Israel, I know that my children also receive the gift of time. We all get this mortal probation, life after death prior to the resurrection, and an additional one thousand years in the millennium. We all get to learn line upon line, precept upon precept, here a little and there a little. God will give us however long it takes for us to get where He needs us to be. I look back on many things that I have endured, my family has endured, and I am amazed how we have gotten through them. I know it is because of the grace of God and the angels that are in our lives both seen and unseen, and if we allow Jesus in our corner, we can all be declared champions.

My blessing also tells me that I will take much joy in my husband and children, and I do. Although it took me a long time to figure out the true meaning of joy, I now understand it. "Adam fell that men might be; and men [and women] are, that they might have joy." ~ *The Book of Mormon 2 Nephi 2:25.*

"The second half of that truth makes clear that we are all here on earth to learn from our experiences and especially to learn how to have joy in our lives. However, the word *might* in that equation indicates that having joy in our lives is not a given. It says that we *might* have joy, not that we will have joy." ~ *Peggy S. Worthen.*

Joy is something we must choose.
Simply put, JOY is:

- Having faith in and a testimony of **J**esus Christ and in His abilities.

- Being **O**bedient and **O**ptimistic.

- **Y**ielding our will to God's and **Y**oking ourselves to Jesus.

However, if you're anything like me, choosing joy is not that simple. Life can be hard, and prior to developing a strong testimony, I allowed my circumstances to dictate my joy and happiness. I wanted life to be smooth and easy, nothing bad or hard to happen. I actually ended up with the opposite of that—but then I am supposed to *choose joy* regardless? How? How do I do that?

Joy has everything to do with our faith and focus. It is a skill to be developed. One that no matter what is happening good or bad in our lives that we keep our eyes fixed on eternal outcomes. We gain an understanding of and maintain our trust in God and His perfect plan of salvation for His children. We keep joy and our circumstances—independent from each other.

I am much better at focusing on Jesus Christ and the plan of happiness, thinking celestial brings me joy. My faith feeds my hope and changes my perspective allowing me to have more grace and choose joy as I interact with my family and others.

Obedience comes easier now than it did before. In the past, I needed to test the boundaries, and I lived on the outside of their safety. Once I decided to become compliant, I remained strictly close to the border, resulting in unnecessary strain and lack of enjoyment. Later, I discovered that God has given me an oversized dance floor to move around on while still remaining disciplined.

Being obedient and making and keeping covenants brings me joy. It does not mean that I escape obstacles or avoid missteps. It just means that I can move confidently with the Lord as my partner knowing He is there to lead and support me.

Optimism is a tricky one. Satan and his influence are all around. We are surrounded by tragedy, bad news, and the evil designs of men and women. However, I stopped watching the news back in 1999. I am not naive to what is going on in the world, but I choose not to focus on it, or bring its negativity into my home. Even with all of the bad in the world, there is still so much good happening all around us—I choose to focus on that.

However, I have not always been the most optimistic person. I still envision worst-case scenarios for myself and imagine that I can survive them; a therapist told me that was a good coping skill. Scott has been such a blessing; he is gifted in this department and has helped me to look for the good every single day, and I am improving.

How we respond to what happens in our life is more important than what actually happens, we get to use our agency to decide. I have had and will continue to have significant opportunities to choose how I will respond to my circumstances and trials. I will continue to choose Jesus Christ. I will continue to choose obedience and increase my optimism. I will continue to have faith and hope.

Yielding our will to God and yoking ourselves to Jesus Christ is easier said than done. We are human in this mortal life and subject to the flesh. For years, I was fixated on what I wanted. What I thought I needed and what I thought my life should look like. Letting go was difficult; trusting God to take full control and learning how to follow rather than lead actually became more empowering and enjoyable. God wants to lead us—let Him!

I will continue to choose to yield and yoke my will, my heart to His because I desire to return home to live with my Father in Heaven and loved ones again someday. Until that day comes, I want joy, and living the gospel brings me joy. My conviction to not give up is strong, and I find comfort knowing that I have got this because God has got me.

I will stay working, moving, and content while anticipating the Lord's promises to be fulfilled. I now understand what my grandma Sue was talking about when she said that I would be *content* with Scott. It does not mean that I settled; it means that I am *in a state of peaceful happiness*, satisfied with what I have, while I wait on the Lord's timing and increased blessings. I know that Scott and I have not arrived, yet, but I have faith in God's plans for us and in our love and willingness to work hard for ourselves and each other. I focus on and trust that the plan of salvation will work. I know that I cannot do everything I used to do, and I am slowly learning that I no longer need to keep my once frantic pace.

Elder Hale taught me that important lesson, "When you cannot do what you have always done, then you only do what matters most." ~ *Elder David A. Bednar of the Quorum of the Twelve Apostles of The Church of Jesus Christ of Latter-day Saints.*

Heavenly Father has been counseling me the last several months to be more of a Mary and less of a Martha. "And Jesus answered and said unto me [Tracy], [Tracy], thou art careful and troubled about many things: But one thing is needful: and [Tracy you need to choose] that good part, which shall not be taken away from [you]." ~ *Holy Bible Luke 10: 41-42.*

I purposefully cut back at work, not to fill that time with being busy, but to fill it with more self-care, reflection, healing, writing, peace, time in the temple, wholeness, and sitting at Jesus's feet. I thought I had chosen the good part a long time ago; so, did Martha. She was busy serving and that was a good thing, don't eliminate that, but Mary knew when it was time to stop what she was doing and sit with and learn from the Savior.

Timing is different for everyone, but right now, in my life, that is what matters most. I encourage you to choose joy and the good part that leads to salvation, there is no greater gift. Your time and efforts in obtaining that gift shall not be taken from you.

In his October of 2010 conference address, Elder Ucht-dorf reminds us of the things that matter most, "... let us be wise. Let us turn to the pure doctrinal waters of the restored gospel... Let us joyfully partake of them in their simplicity and plainness. The heavens are open again. The gospel of Jesus Christ is on earth once more, and its simple truths are a plentiful source of joy! ...Indeed, we have great reason to rejoice. If life and its rushed pace and many stresses have made it difficult for you to feel like rejoicing, then perhaps now is a good time to refocus...Strength comes not from frantic activity but from being settled on a firm foundation of truth and light. It comes from placing our attention and efforts on the basics...it comes from paying attention to the divine things [they] matter most."

It can be hard to stay centered on the divine, all of the time. It can be hard when we are in the middle of a trial or buried under a pile of crap to see, feel, and choose joy. Life gets in the way, and we can lose our focus. If we commit to being and doing good, we will not get too far off the path. If we can just inch ahead, remembering that direction is more important than speed.

We were recently reminded that "Because of the redeeming life and mission of our Savior, Jesus Christ, we can—and should—be the most joyful people on earth!" *~ Elder Patrick Kearon of the Quorum of the Twelve Apostles of The Church of Jesus Christ of Latter-day Saints.*

CHAPTER TWENTY-SIX

All is Well

AVING REALIZED when I started my book, I set a goal to have it wrapped up and fully written on exactly the two-year mark, and two-thirds was written in just three short months. I asked my husband to find something to do so I could have the day to finalize, and I thought I had finished, minus the major edits. I was ready in time for the adult session of Stake Conference that same evening. The Spirit at the meeting was strong, and I was once again reminded that everyone has challenges and struggles. I know this to be true, some hide or handle their difficulties better than others, but we all have them. Just because we keep coming to church, for some of us that does not mean we are okay. I knew that I needed to add one more chapter to my book.

I'm not even sure if I can call it my book as I have had the aid and inspiration of the Spirit in the several ways that revelation is received. I have had to relive many hard things and even argued with Heavenly Father about content that I was reluctant to include. Eventually, I succumbed to His will and, as a result, added several vulnerable experiences. My faith lies with God and His secret reason for their inclusion. I live in a small community, and if this book ever gets published, my extended family, friends, neighbors, co-workers, and ward family are going to learn all the things about me, and several things about my family. It makes me nervous and scared, but I have received confirmation that all will be well.

During the Stake Conference, we were invited to learn our identity, find our purpose, and to evaluate how much time we are spending on frivolous activities that have no value. Be more productive, find balance, and look for ways to help others. When we are baptized, we enter into a ministering covenant to bear one another's burdens, mourn with those that mourn, comfort others, serve Him, and keep the commandments. The two greatest are to love God and to love others as ourselves. We were asked to be more intentional and to participate in the most important work, that of gathering Israel on both sides of the veil. We were encouraged to stay on the covenant path and help others find and stay there so that we can all make our way back home.

A theme that kept coming up was that of music. It was mentioned how the lyrics for the conference were carefully selected and provided direction for the assigned topics. The stake president included in one of his talks, the hymn written by William Clayton, "Come, Come, Ye Saints." Several speakers reminded us that music is a conduit to the Spirit, and that music helps us feel God's love.

I recalled a general conference address from 2015 titled, "The Music of the Gospel." "Yea, behold, I will tell you in your mind and in your heart, by the Holy Ghost, which shall come upon you and which shall dwell in your heart…We learn the dance steps with our minds, but we hear the music with our hearts. The dance steps of the gospel are the things we do; the music of the gospel is the joyful spiritual feeling that comes from the Holy Ghost. It brings a change of heart and is the source of all righteous desires. The dance steps require discipline, but the joy of the dance will be experienced only when we come to hear the music." ~ *Elder Wilford W. Andersen of the Seventy of The Church of Jesus Christ of Latter-day Saints.*

I liken that talk to the letter of the law and the love of the law. Many are obedient and know all of the do's and don'ts of gospel living. They know the ideal steps, they go through the motions, they can perform the routine. Others can feel the music and like to freestyle dance without learning the exact steps. Those who prefer their dance often judge other members for not following the same choreography. I would like to propose that there are several dance routines to choose from according to our circumstances. We may not all be able to perform the same number. I think God is happy when we get up and move, only then can He direct our feet. However, we are to learn the basic steps and incorporate them into our routine, while simultaneously hearing and feeling the music. In order to do that we must be in tune with the Spirit, or what Elder Wilford W. Anderson calls "...aligning with the correct frequency."

Can you imagine if each of us were in tune enough to hear, therefore feel the music of the gospel, while performing one of the many diverse dance numbers on beat and in step. On top of that, if we added the buoyancy we can develop, through learning how to let the gospel carry us, we would be at ease and light on our feet.

If you google "light on your feet," it will offer many definitions: The phrase suggests that the dancers are able to move easily and with grace, without seeming overly heavy or burdened by their weight. "Light on their feet" also implies agility and the ability to move quickly and accurately. Achieving this lightness often requires a combination of strength, flexibility, and the ability to transfer weight and momentum effectively.

Are we hearing the beautiful, inspiring, influential gospel music, is it motivating us to sing, dance, and rejoice? If we are not, let's ask ourselves, what changes do we need to make? We might even ask God if there is more fitting choreography for our circumstances. "If thou art [joyful], praise the Lord with singing, with music, with dancing, and with a prayer of praise and thanksgiving." ~ *Doctrine & Covenants 136: 28.*

Another common theme from Stake Conference was that everyone deals with hard things, but through the challenges and struggles, we can still pray and feel the prayers of others on our behalf. We can have the ministering of angels. We can still receive tender mercies, amid our struggles. We can always turn to God. We can communicate with our Heavenly Father and learn how He communicates with us, because He speaks every language. We can remember that all good comes from God and to just keep doing the next right thing. And regardless of how much we go through or how much we seemingly get fertilizer heaped upon us, through the atonement of Jesus Christ, we can be washed clean.

I thought of another conference talk, "Mortality Works!" Elder Hales recounts his challenges and the challenges of others. He counsels, "When we feel distraught or anxious about our problems or feel that we might be receiving more than our fair share of life's difficulties, we can remember what the Lord said to the children of Israel: "And thou shalt remember all the way[s] which the Lord thy God led thee these forty years in the wilderness, to humble thee, and to prove thee, to

know what [is] in thine heart, whether thou [would] keep his commandments, or no." And so, we should not be surprised when hard times come upon us. We will encounter situations that try us and people who enable us to practice true charity and patience. But we need to bear up under our difficulties…"
~ *Elder Brook P. Hales of the Seventy of The Church of Jesus Christ of Latter-day Saints.*

Are we bearing up, are we facing our difficulties with strength, courage, joy, and rejoicing? Are we determined to succeed and endure? For years, I stayed buried under my heavy load, it almost crushed me. I could not see a way out from under it.

However, Elder Bednar reminds us that it is the very load that provides the life-saving traction that enables us to get unstuck, to get back on the path, press forward, and return to our family and our home. We are promised that the Savior will help us to bear up our burdens with ease. ~ Elder David A. Bednar *of the Quorum of the Twelve Apostles of The Church of Jesus Christ of Latter-day Saints.*

Bearing a heavy load is part of mortality. "Brothers and sisters, mortality works! It is designed to work! Despite the challenges, heartaches, and difficulties we all face, our loving, wise, and perfect Heavenly Father has designed the plan of happiness such that we are not destined to fail." ~ *Elder Brook P. Hales of the Seventy of The Church of Jesus Christ of Latter-day Saints.*

"Fear not to do good, my sons, [and daughters] for whatsoever ye sow, that shall ye also reap; therefore, if ye sow good ye shall also reap good for your reward. Therefore, fear not, little flock; do good; let earth and hell combine against you, for if ye are built upon my rock, they cannot prevail. Look unto me in every thought; doubt not, fear not." ~ *Doctrine & Covenants 6:33-34, 36.*

I love that God has designed a perfect plan for His children, for you and for me, that if we build on His rock, His foundation we cannot fall and we will not fail.

We have all been wounded, hurt, or broken. In his talk "When Things Don't Go as Planned," Jack R Christianson emphasized that God knows all things and there isn't anything save He knows it. So, if we don't get the job or promotion we wanted, if our prayers are not answered the way we think they should be. If God does not come running to succor us, to spare us, to stop or intervene, or immediately heal us, "then we better know that there is a darn good reason." Because God is not in the habit of making His children unnecessarily suffer. ~ *Jack R Christianson.*

The scriptures list the many ways in which we could possibly suffer, then God provides us His reasoning for allowing us to do so. "...and above all, if the very jaws of hell shall gape open the mouth wide after thee, know thou, my [sons and daughters], that all these things shall give thee experience, and shall be for thy good. The Son of Man hath descended below them all. Art thou greater than He? ...Thy days are known, and thy years shall not be numbered less; therefore, fear not what man can do, for God shall be with you forever and ever." ~ *Doctrine & Covenants 122: 7-9.*

Because the Savior suffered all things unto death, He knows how to succor us in our infirmities.

One speaker during the Stake Conference referenced the talk, "Ponder The Path of Thy Feet." "As we look to Jesus as our Exemplar and as we follow in His footsteps, we can return safely to our Heavenly Father to live with Him forever. Jesus walked,

... through many of the same challenges we…face in life. Jesus walked the path of disappointment, temptation, pain, He was "in an agony … and His sweat was as it were great drops of blood falling down to the ground." And none can forget His suffering on the cruel cross. …While we will find on our path bitter sorrow, we can also find great happiness. We, with Jesus, can walk [or dance] the path of obedience, service and prayer."
~ *President Thomas S. Monson, former president of The Church of Jesus Christ of Latter-day Saints.*

I started holding my breath again, waiting to finish this chapter, keeping space for the possibility that something worthy of writing about could take place over the next few months. A lot can happen in a short amount of time. I have had three precancerous adenomas removed within a nine-month time span, they are growing fast, possibly because of all the extra fertilizer I have been receiving lately. Where my mind likes to go is the worst-case scenario of course.

I pray all of the time and say to Heavenly Father, *if something is going to happen, I need you to prepare me and help me through it.* Recently, the thought entered my mind, *you have already been prepared, and I will continue to help you through everything, as I always have.*

It is true that something could happen, and chances are they will. It may not be that my worst fears play out, it could be that my greatest hopes and dreams come true, or that I will get to participate in many of the great and stirring events preparatory to the second coming.

Regardless of what actually happens, I know what the answers are, or I will know where to find them. I know what the final result will be, that I will endure whatever it is the best I can and continue to choose joy. I have tools at my disposal; I have a strong testimony of all the things I have written in this book. My greatest desire used to be that I would be loved, and that I would be enough. My desires have changed. They now include that I will always be able to feel the love that is already there for me and to remember that I have always been and will always be enough, no matter what happens. Because of Christ's atonement, it is not possible for me to fall short. I will continue returning to the mount often, seeking guidance and direction from the Lord. I will continue to watch for my rainbow, and my promised blessings. "I will glory in my strength and infirmities that the power of Christ may rest upon me." ~ *Holy Bible 2 Corinthians 12: 9.*

My righteous desires also include the ability to use my voice for good. I have always been guarded, and I want to lower my guard and carefully welcome new friends in. I want to be bold, brave, serve, help, and lift others. I want to remind people that yes, life is hard, but you will get through it, trust the Lord and use the strengthening enabling power of Christ. Keep inching forward, keep serving others and doing good works, if you put in the effort, you will be generously rewarded. Do not let your troubles, fears, doubts, or religion weigh you down; find your wings. I want to help people learn to dance, feel the music, love, and enjoy the gospel as much as I do. I want everyone to understand that whatever happens in your life, there is a darn good reason for it. And please know that because of God's great plan, eventually, all will be well.

Prod·i·gal

A person who leaves home and behaves recklessly, but later makes a repentant return.

CHAPTER TWENTY-SEVEN

My Return

*L*IKE THE PRODIGAL SON, I did not comprehend that home already consisted of everything that I would need to be successful. I had my father's kingdom and His inheritance at my disposal. The answers were right in front of me, but I was blind and could not see. My Heavenly Father was there, helping me, but I did not recognize His hand before I left His protection and care. Jesus was in my dreams as a little girl, holding me, reassuring me that everything would be okay. The Spirit was with me when our family was sealed, ensuring lasting feelings that would later draw me back to the temple. My sister was sent to sit on my bed only a few days after her passing to let me know she was all right.

God used that poster on my wall to remind me that He did not make junk. Following my departure, I was still encouraged to just keep moving, through music and dance. Later, I recognized divine intervention with graduating from high school and other educational opportunities. God carefully placed people in my life, angels in the form of family, friends, co-workers, and others that have helped me. He calmed the waters as I struggled through the storms of life. He was always at the edge of the darkness I ventured into on more than one occasion. First being when I got mad at Him and moved far away.

Only after depleting my self-worth and inheritance did I come to myself. I knew that the only way I was going to survive was if I humbly begged to move back home. I was afraid that He might not accept me, but He was still there, right where He had always been, waiting with outstretched arms until I decided to return. Even after He welcomed me back, I contemplated whether or not to stick around. I never fully unpacked while I was trying to figure things out in the beginning, throughout my second divorce, and the first several years of Scott's and my marriage. I eventually committed and fully unpacked. I decided that with my physical and mental illness, trauma and trials, no other doctor or hospital would do, Jesus Christ is the master physician and healer. I knew that no one or nothing could offer more assistance in dealing with my several obstacles, infirmities, and storms.

Because I had left home before, I knew what it was like out in the world, alone, on my own, and in the dark. I never wanted to go back to that comfortless place, not even for a visit. I would only like to apologize for the harm that I caused while there. Like the apostle Peter, I pondered, where else would I go. For my father and brother, Jesus Christ, have all the words of eternal life. ~ *Holy Bible John 6:68.*

Eventually, I believed, had faith, and accepted that the entirety of His beautiful plan of happiness was and is true. So, I choose to stay living at home, to stay in the safety of living the gospel and in making and keeping covenants. Returning home did not and does not take away my trials and problems. It only gets me through them better. It provided and still provides me with needed assistance.

Every priesthood blessing, sacrament, and temple ordnance, every angel dispatched on my behalf have given me succor and strength. I have been able to develop my gifts, talents, increase my education, manage my disappointments, disabilities, opportunities, and adventures. I have found meaning and purpose in every calling, job, chapter, every detail of my entire life's journey. I realized without returning, my life would be very different right now. I want to be home, within His reach. I want Him sustaining me, holding my hand, carrying me, guiding me, teaching me, walking with me, tutoring me, loving me, trusting me to do, and helping me with my part. When I am home, I get to wear my father's robe, it is symbolic of the atonement, it covers me. Jesus Christ and His atoning sacrifice makes me more than I could ever be on my own. It empowers me. It allows me to be saved from physical death and gives me a chance for salvation and exaltation through my faithfulness.

I had a hard time writing my life story, sharing my journey, my return. It was difficult to describe with the same level of intensity the thoughts and feelings that I had at the time those events took place. I have grown, learned, healed, and forgiven. I found myself questioning if my life was really as hard as I remember. I concluded that *yes it was*. My experiences were real, they were intense, they were painful and hard at the time. I did not know everything I know now. I didn't have all of the information, so my thoughts, feelings, and beliefs were developed accordingly. I am grateful that I can look back and see all the tender mercies, the hidden treasures that I did not recognize at the time. I am grateful that I survived it. I have done hard things. I will continue to do hard things knowing that Heavenly Father and the Savior love me, and with the aid of the Holy Ghost along with heavenly and earthly angels, they will always assist me, if I let them. I know that one of those guardian angels is my sister.

I have experienced revelation and the Spirit in the many ways it can be received. I have not always understood the inspiration, instruction, or the direction it was giving me, but it was there. It took time for all of the pieces to come together. Other times have been so clear and discernible that I cannot unknow it. I desire to love and lift others. In order to do that, I can't live in fear that people will judge me, my feelings, or my experiences. I know that I am not for everyone and that's okay. I am for the people that can see through my hurt, anger, pain, poor judgments, my riotous living, my learning, and see the growth, healing, love, forgiveness, grace, charity, and the light that I have received through the healing and saving power of the atonement of Jesus Christ.

I agree with Elder Holland's assessment in that I can show gratitude and thank my Father in Heaven because I was allowed to change. I thank Jesus, He is the reason I can change, and "ultimately we do so only with Their divine assistance." Not everything I have struggled with was a result of my own actions. Some things were the "result of the actions of others or just the mortal events of life." ~ *Elder Jeffrey R. Holland of the Quorum of the Twelve Apostles of The Church of Jesus Christ of Latter-day Saints.*

However, I have changed the things that I can, or I am still actively working on it. As far as everything else, the things I can't change, I have chosen to forgive. I have let them go and joyfully leave them in the hands of God.

I had to learn how to trust in the Lord without knowing the outcomes. I love the Lord and know that He still loves me regardless of what the outcomes actually are, and whether or not they are favorable. I know that God turns all things, the good, bad, and ugly, for our profit. God has proved to me that when He asks me to let go, even of the things that I like or love, it creates space for Him to give me more. He always replaces what I thought was good with something better or best. I do not want to hang on to what I want. I am in His hands.

What I desire more than anything is what God wants for me.

When I returned and really started getting active again in my home ward, I felt like I had a prodigal "older brother," in my case sisters, that looked down on me. I thought I could feel their glares, questioning my return and worthiness to receive gospel blessings and inheritance. Early on, I boldly stood in Relief Society and bore my testimony.

I said, "I feel that some of you look at me as if I should not be here. But I do not come for you, I come for me, and I know that I deserve to be here just as much as anyone else. I know that God loves me and that I belong."

After that meeting, one seemingly glaring sister came up to me and expressed her happiness for my return and welcomed me back. That interaction taught me a lot. Just because we think it, does not make it true, and what God thinks of us is always more important than the opinions, or perceived opinions of others.

If you have moved away, are considering leaving, or are longing for love, home, and family, please return, stay, or join us. Heavenly Father and Jesus love you and will assist you. They want to give you treasures and restore your inheritance; it is Their decision to make. Some may unrighteously judge, let them. I am here, and others like me, many will rejoice in your presence. We can help until you feel comfortable enough to fully unpack your bags and remind you that you are not alone. Whatever your struggles, regardless of why you moved, why you are compilating leaving, or your reasons for not joining sooner, it is never too late for you to come home. God is home, He is here watching, waiting to wrap you in the robe of Christ's atonement, His love—it covers ALL, decide to be ALL in.

I add my invitation and testimony with that of Elder Palmer. "There is hope even when all seems lost." To all who are longing for faith, we invite you to come back... I promise your faith can be strengthened as you once again worship with the Saints... We invite you to come back so you can once again taste the joyous fruit of the gospel...This message is not a challenge, and it is not a condemnation. It is an invitation, extended with love and a sincere desire to welcome you back to your spiritual home...[We] have prayed that you will feel the witness of the Holy Ghost as you now hear this loving invitation and magnificent promise from our Savior, Jesus Christ: "Will ye not now return unto me, and repent of your sins, and be converted, that I may heal you?" ...The journey back is often not easy or comfortable, but it is worth it... Be patient as your faith and testimony grow. Through the Atonement of Jesus Christ, all that is broken can be healed." ~ *Elder S. Mark Palmer of the Presidency of the Seventy of The Church of Jesus Christ of Latter-day Saints.*

I stand as a witness as I have learned for myself that The Church of Jesus Christ of Latter- day Saints is true. I know it contains the keys of the priesthood, the fullness and the ordinances necessary for eternal life. It is the complete package. I testify that God the Father and His only begotten son live, that They love us more than we can comprehend. I know that the Holy Ghost provides peace, comfort, truth, and inspiration that will help us navigate and find our path. I know that all things will eventually be turned for our good, growth, and learning.

"If ye can no more than desire to believe," exercising just "a particle of faith," giving even a small place for the promises of God to find a home—that is enough to begin." Elder Holland also asks, "Are you battling a demon of addiction—tobacco or drugs or gambling, or the pernicious contemporary plague of pornography? Is your marriage in trouble or your child in danger? Are you confused with gender identity or searching for self-esteem? Do you, or someone you love, face disease or depression or death? Whatever other steps you may need to take to resolve these concerns, come first to the gospel of Jesus Christ. Trust in heaven's promises. In that regard Alma's testimony is my testimony: "I do know," he says, "that whosoever shall put their trust in God shall be supported in their trials, and their troubles, and their afflictions." This reliance upon the merciful nature of God is at the very center of the gospel Christ taught." ~ *Elder Jeffrey R. Holland of the Quorum of the Twelve Apostles of The Church of Jesus Christ of Latter-day Saints.*

I testify that I have been supported in my messes, trials, troubles, and afflictions, you can be too. Please know that there are many waiting with outstretched arms in heaven and on earth to welcome you home. We are ready to sing, dance, and rejoice in your return. Eager for you to experience the love, forgiveness, peace, and joy that can only be found through the enabling power of the atonement of Jesus Christ, in His name I dedicate and consecrate my life, my time, my talents, and my desires, Amen

... Godspeed

Afterword

THE ONE PERSON I used to compare myself to is my big sister, Terri. She radiates with greatness and iridescent beauty. Upon comparison, I fell short. When I was born, everyone was required to ask her permission to hold me because I was "her" baby. She always took very good care of me; she still does. She is my Guardian Angel. Our relationship might be considered out of the ordinary.

I used to be her shy, backward, dark shadow, inclined to go undetected, although she always noticed me, hiding. She was often annoyed with my attempts to be like her and with her. She eventually found a place that I could not trail behind as heaven would not allow me to follow her there.

When Terri died, I was immediately thrust into the additional position of oldest child. Trying to fill her shoes was an overwhelming task with impossible expectations. I soon realized that I would never be able to fill her shoes. I regretfully continued to stumble around in them for years.

Terri made it known that I would be all right on my own, but I was convinced that I would never be okay without her. Terri was the peacemaker in our home. When she left, what family harmony we had followed. Terri was a person everyone enjoyed being around, filled with love, light, and laughter.

Others were drawn to her inner glow as she illuminated any room with her personality. Terri keeps me grounded on the straight and narrow and gently guiding me along.

Terri is always there for me. When I need her, she arrives immediately; she is never detained when rushing to my aid. I can talk to her about anything without fear. She is a great sounding board; she never interrupts and allows me to arrive at self-resolution. My sister has always encouraged me to be a better person. Her shining example provides a lighted path that I can parallel, not duplicate, at my own pace.

I realized that one of the greatest gifts I received as a result of her passing was the eventual desire to step out of the shadows and be me. It took years, but I have found purpose in life, more understanding in death, desires to seek for knowledge, wisdom, and joy. She continues to cultivate a longing in me to improve. I know that she is always near me watching over me, strengthening and enlightening me. I know that I will be with her again. I believed that she left me behind, but that has never been true, she has always been with me, helping God carry me through.

In Loving Memory

Of my Guardian ANGEL

TERRI LYNNE WALKER

9-10-1970 / 9-30-1985

www.ingramcontent.com/pod-product-compliance
Lightning Source LLC
Chambersburg PA
CBHW071716120626

46550CB00001B/257